Money Before Marriage

Following God's Blueprint for Financial Stewardship

Pastor John F. Ramsey Sr.

Copyright © 2020 by **John F. Ramsey Sr.**

All rights reserved. No part of this publication may be reproduced, distributed, or transmitted in any form or by any means, without prior written permission.

Unless otherwise noted, all Scripture quotations are taken from the New American Standard Bible ® (NASB), copyright © 1960, 1962, 1963, 1968, 1971, 1972, 1973, 1975, 1977, 1995 by The Lockman Foundation. Used by permission. www.Lockman.org.

Scripture quotations marked (ASV) are taken from the American Standard Version (Revised Version, Standard American Edition of the Bible). 1900, 1901, 1929. Public Domain.

Scripture quotations marked (ESV) are taken from The ESV® Bible (The Holy Bible, English Standard Version®) copyright © 2001 by Crossway, a publishing ministry of Good News Publishers. ESV® Text Edition: 2011. The ESV® text has been reproduced in cooperation with and by permission of Good News Publishers. Unauthorized reproduction of this publication is prohibited. Used by permission. All rights reserved.

Scripture quotations marked (NIV) are taken from the Holy Bible, New International Version. Copyright © 1973, 1978, 1984, 2011 by Biblica, Inc.® Used by permission. All rights reserved worldwide.

Scripture quotations marked (NLT) are taken from the Holy Bible, New Living Translation, copyright © 1996, 2004, 2015 by Tyndale House Foundation. Used by permission of Tyndale House Publishers, Inc., Carol Stream, Illinois 60188. All rights reserved.

Sermon To Book
www.sermontobook.com

Money Before Marriage / John F. Ramsey Sr.
ISBN-13: 978-1-952602-01-6

"Relevant" and "practical" are but a couple of the words that describe this timely book by Pastor John Ramsey. He masterfully explains the importance of having and handling money before marriage from a biblical context, while challenging couples to be fiscally disciplined and responsible. This is a must read for any couple seriously considering marriage.
Bishop Joseph Warren Walker, III
International Presiding Bishop, Full Gospel Baptist Church Fellowship
Senior Pastor, Mount Zion Baptist Church Nashville

CONTENTS

Foreword by Bishop Joseph Warren Walker III 3
Good Stewards 5
Get Your Money Straight 9
Money, Marriage, and Financial Stability 29
Dealing with Debt 53
Rapid Debt Reduction 77
Building a Financial Future 93
Maintaining Financial Freedom 113
Financial Freedom 123
About the Author 125
Notes 128

Foreword by Bishop Joseph Warren Walker III

Marriage is more than the merger of two lives—it is the collision of two histories. Often those histories include a litany of regrettable decisions. How we have or have not handled money has a tremendous impact upon marriage. When God brings us together into a covenant relationship of marriage, we must be committed to working together to accomplish the purposes He has designed for our lives. John Ramsey has given us a needed resource that addresses the problem that has plagued many marriages before they even get out of the gate.

I've seen so many couples skirt around the issue of money, assuming that it will all come together after they say, "I do." Nothing could be further from the truth. This book is a prayer answered because it provides practical tools for couples to have this important conversation.

Ramsey has masterfully given us a roadmap in navigating the terrain of financial literacy. In the book of

Genesis, God told Adam and Eve to be fruitful and multiply. It was clear that they were to produce fruit or be productive in every area of their lives before they multiplied. This is the divine order of God. If we are not fruitful, we end up multiplying dysfunction, which opens the door to generational curses.

Financial illiteracy can be passed down to your children and your children's children. It has always been God's desire—as stated in Proverbs 13:22—that a "good man leaves an inheritance to his children's children." When we commit to getting our money in order before we come into marriage relationships, we enter into the union from a place of wholeness.

I'm so excited about this book. It is with great detail and spiritual genius that John Ramsey has given us all a resource that every couple serious about accomplishing God's will in the earth together needs to read. I highly recommend this resource. There is much God wants us to accomplish in marriage, and it takes a good relationship—not only with each other, but also with money.

Bishop Joseph Warren Walker III
Int. Presiding, Bishop Full Gospel Baptist Church Fellowship
Senior Pastor, Mount Zion Baptist Church Nashville

INTRODUCTION

Good Stewards

Many Americans are entangled in their finances and in serious debt because of poor planning. Financial problems not only cause individual stress, but they also are a major factor in the break-ups of marriages and families. I feel so passionately about financial literacy—having knowledge and information to manage our money and spending—because, after thirty years of ministry, I have seen families, marriages, friendships, businesses, and lives destroyed because of unwise money management choices. Poor financial stewardship is directly related to instability and insecurity in our lives. Therefore, if we increase our discipline and knowledge, we increase our odds of making sound financial decisions and living a life of freedom and security.

We need to understand God is not only concerned with our spiritual wellbeing—as Christians, our names are written in the Lamb's Book of Life (Revelation 21:27)—but also our physical wellbeing. He wants us to make it while we are on this earth. In John 10:10, Jesus said, "I came that they may have life, and have it abundantly." Not being able to pay your bills is not an abundant life. It's one thing for God to bless us, but it's another to have the discipline to manage that blessing. He wants us to be good stewards—good managers—of the gifts He has given us and not to waste or misuse them.

Most Christians do not realize there are 2,300 references on money management and stewardship in the Bible.[1] The subject of money dominates many of Jesus' teachings and parables in the New Testament, as well as the epistles of Paul and other writers. It's a subject God cares about, so we should care about it, too.

If the Bible is God's blueprint for daily living, then you should read it and use it as a daily step-by-step approach to become a vessel of Christian stewardship and gain financial freedom. With this book, I'm hoping to show you some scriptural principles and apply them to your life, especially relating to your marriage and family or the marriage you desire to have. If you do so, you will experience true financial freedom.

We will address this in practical ways throughout this book, and at the end of each chapter, workbook sections will help you apply these tools of financial stewardship to your life.

Before we start, it's important to have a biblical understanding of some basic financial terms I will use throughout this book. How the world defines them and how God defines them is often different, and we want to make sure we follow God's definition if we want financial freedom.

Debt is owing somebody something beyond your

current ability to repay it. There is nothing wrong with having some debt, but our goal must be to pay off all debt. Romans 13:8 says, "Owe nothing to anyone except to love one another."

It has become so normal in our culture to take on debt that most people can't relate to this. But I want you to think about your future. I want to shatter some of those old paradigms of thinking it's normal to live from hand to mouth. That is not God's best for your life. When I sow seed, God might be responsible for my harvest, but I'm responsible for my stewardship.

Surety in the Bible means co-signing or becoming responsible for somebody else's debt if they cannot pay it back. Some Bible translations call this being a *guarantor*. This is something you never want to do for anybody! If the banks won't give them credit, there's a reason!

Work is a gift from God. Exodus 20:9 says, "Six days you shall labor and do all your work." God designed us for work, and it was part of the Ten Commandments. Therefore, work is part of God's plan for prosperity.

Some people have a negative attitude about work. No matter how holy you think you are, if you've got a nasty attitude every time you go to work, your attitude is canceling the benefits of God. When God created Adam and Eve, He placed them in the garden of Eden. Before Eve showed up, God placed Adam in the garden to work (Genesis 2:15). Sin didn't show up until Genesis 3, meaning that work is part of His will for your life and not a result of the fall.

If you're broke, sometimes you have to take the less-than-ideal job with less-than-ideal circumstances. If you're broke, you can't sit back and talk about what you're *not* going to do. There's a great place to go when you need some money, and that's work.

Additionally, you've got to stop spending more than you receive from your paycheck because that's how you get in trouble. You must learn to be content with your current financial status rather than trying to keep up with cultural pressure to have *more*. What you have in this world has no power to change the truth of God's Word, but applying the wisdom from His Word has the power to change your circumstances. When you follow God's blueprint for financial stewardship, you will be blessed.

Are you ready for God to make some changes to your financial situation? It will require discipline and wisdom. If you want to gain knowledge and you're ready to follow through with the hard things, then let's begin.

CHAPTER ONE

Get Your Money Straight

As Americans, we are a nation in debt. Poverty is out of control. According to the most recent figures from the Federal Reserve Board, United States consumer debt is $13.67 trillion.[2] This figure, when compared to the median income of $60,366 in American households[3] and current poverty levels—13.4 percent of the 2017 U.S. population[4]—is appalling. Consumer debt is crippling our lives, and in many instances, has made it almost impossible for us to move out of our paralyzed lifestyles. And when you bring money problems and bad financial habits into marriage, it is a recipe for disaster. God not only has a plan for your life, but He also has a plan for your finances.

Control Your Finances

Make no mistake—to control your life, you must control your finances. You must learn to properly manage money to correct your finances and become debt-free. It takes more than consolidating your bills into one monthly payment. While this may be a good start, you must educate yourself on the basic principles of eliminating debt and building savings for your future. This is the first step to financial stability. Throughout this book, we will explore biblical approaches to becoming financially secure.

You cannot build a sturdy house without a firm foundation (Luke 6:48), and you cannot build anything without the right tools for the job. The same logic applies to your finances. We live in a society that gives us the freedom to make choices. However, some choices are creating havoc in our lives. Regarding finances, it's possible to make one bad decision and spend the next ten years trying to undo the consequences of that decision.

We Want It All, and We Want It Now!

We live in a culture that's built on instant gratification—everyone wants everything now. The problem with many Christians is they bring that mentality into the house of God when they get saved. So now they're saved and on the right side of eternity, but they're living out their salvation, thinking everything God promised them will happen right now. It's time to be delivered from that.

I want you to know patience is part of the process. In our culture, many of us would rather look like we're wealthy than exercise the principles it takes to accumulate wealth. The Bible says, "Wealth gained hastily will dwindle, but whoever gathers little by little will increase it" (Proverbs 13:11 ESV). So, the increase comes over time. I believe the Bible is true. If you can exercise patience and live below your means now, you can increase your means and your lifestyle later on.

When I started my first church, I was making a little over $200 a week and had two college diplomas. But I still saved $50 every week. (Athletic scholarships paid for my college.) I gave to God by paying my tithes, I worked out my bills with the rest, and I put a couple of dollars in my pocket. I was intentional in being a good steward of the money I had to work with. The Bible says a lot about stewardship and the mistakes we make when our priorities aren't straight.

The Parable of the Unrighteous Steward

> *Now He was also saying to the disciples, "There was a rich man who had a manager, and this manager was reported to him as squandering his possessions. And he called him and said to him, 'What is this I hear about you? Give an accounting of your management, for you can no longer be manager.' the manager said to himself, 'What shall I do, since my master is taking the management away from me? I am not strong enough to dig; I am ashamed to beg. I know what I shall do, so that when I am removed from the management people will welcome me into their homes.'*
>
> *And he summoned each one of his master's debtors, and he began saying to the first, 'How much do you owe my master?' And he said, 'A hundred measures of oil.' And he said to him, 'Take your bill, and sit down quickly and write fifty.' Then he said to another, 'And how much do you owe?' And he said, 'A hundred measures of wheat.' He said to him, 'Take your bill, and write eighty.' And his master praised the unrighteous manager because he had acted shrewdly;*

> *for the sons of this age are more shrewd in relation to their own kind than the sons of light.*
> —**Luke 16:1–8**

In this parable, the man who had just received his job evaluation was about to be fired because the evaluation revealed he was ineffective. We can look at this parable as an example of how the creativity of his manager allowed him to stay afloat financially. That's what Jesus was commending—not his dishonesty, but his creativity. He thought of ways to survive, knowing that if he didn't, he would be unemployed. Scripture says that this man acted shrewdly. But the job that you do is not only evaluated by your boss, it is also evaluated by God.

The *ESV Study Bible* explains it this way:[5]

> [The main point of the parable] is that the manager had great foresight to anticipate his financial needs after his dismissal, thus using his financial expertise to make friends for himself.... Jesus applies this parable both as a comparison and a contrast. In contrast to the manager, Jesus' disciples must not use their money unrighteously, but like the manager they must use their money in such a way that they prepare for their future life.

When we don't have all the money we want or need, God expects us to be creative and responsible with what He's given us. We can't expect God to increase our wealth when we are irresponsible and making bad choices. The result of this type of behavior is still the same—insufficient funds.

Your Money Habits Reveal Who You Are

The way you handle money tells the world a lot about your personal character and how you handle your life overall. Your life will look like your financial habits—you waste it, or you spend it and invest it. And when you bring those financial habits and character traits into a marriage and family, the people closest to you will be affected the most by them.

So what does your money say about you? Are you a selfish person or a generous person? Are you prideful, or are you walking in humility? Do you act on impulses, or are you self-controlled? Do you rely on your strength and knowledge, or do you trust in God's strength and wisdom?

Your answers to these questions about your financial habits will tell you a lot about yourself and where your priorities lie and will give you clues about how that might work out in a marriage and family. Unfortunately, too many people have bad financial habits and character flaws, and the problems we see in our culture today reveal that sad reality.

Generally, people make four common mistakes with their finances: overspending, failing to prepare for their future, living paycheck to paycheck, and borrowing until payday. Let's look at each of these more closely.

1. Overspending

Overspending is purchasing unnecessary items. When you overspend, you do not balance your needs (food, shelter, and clothing) and desires (upgraded wheels for your car, countless pairs of fancy shoes, and the latest cell phone) with your resources (wages, tips, and savings). Some people go to the mall and know before they go into the store that they cannot afford to shop there but do it anyway.

This is destructive behavior. When we make reckless purchases and spend money we don't have or cannot repay—it is the same as stealing. We are then poor stewards of what God provides. Second Timothy 2:22 warns us of seeking after youthful lusts, "But flee youthful lusts, and follow after righteousness, faith, love, peace, with them that call on the Lord out of a pure heart" (ASV).

Often, people abuse government assistance and use it as an excuse to perpetuate poor financial stewardship. While God may see fit to use government aid to help through an unexpected, strenuous time—until you can stabilize your finances—government assistance should not become your cure-all or a crutch to enable your poor choices. God wants to be your source. He wants you to depend on Him to provide for you, and He has given you the tools you need to turn your financial situation around.

You need to develop biblical discipline to control your spending and maintain your resources.

2. Failing To Prepare for Your Future

Many people get so caught up in enjoying the moment that they fail to prepare for their future. This is related to overspending. You buy unnecessary items to increase your enjoyment of the next two days, starting on Friday after work. You visit the barber or beauty salon, get a manicure or pedicure, buy a new watch, get a shoeshine, or buy the new suit you saw earlier this week to wear to your Saturday event. But you can't afford these items.

You spend a large portion of your income maximizing an image to impress people. If you continually try to "keep up with the Joneses," you will never get ahead financially.

Instead, God calls you to be content with your current situation. Being content is a learned behavior. Contentment does not mean you are satisfied. It means you are appreciative and thankful for your current level until you get to the next level.

One key point to obtaining financial security is to take a step-by-step approach until you are living within your means and preparing for your future.

Too many people believe Social Security is all they will need for their futures and for retirement. But I think it should be renamed "Social Insecurity." I told my wife, "If Social Security is still available when I retire, it will be gas money for us." Social Security isn't enough for people to retire on. You need to have a plan so you aren't left with mere pennies when you retire.

Wouldn't it be wonderful if, instead of relying on a Social Security check in your retirement, you lived responsibly and paid off all your debt and had a substantial retirement set up for yourself? If you plan wisely and can have $80,000 a year in retirement (combined from Social Security, investments, savings, and other retirement funds), and your house and major debts are paid off—this will set you free to not only enjoy your retirement but to use it to bless others. When you get your retirement paycheck, you will be able to think, *"Okay, God, what do you want me to do? Who's getting blessed this week?"* because you won't be weighed down and bound by financial strain and debt. Isn't that a better way of spending your money? When we have resources, we have options; when we don't, then other people and systems determine our options.

Staring a retirement account does not have to be complicated. When I started my retirement account, trust me, I didn't have enough to be complicated in my process. My advice is to go simple until you learn more about other options you may have. When I started my first church, I had little support and there was no system in place, so I created my own. I went to my bank with $100 and told my banker I needed a simple Individual Retirement Account (IRA), and each month, I deposited $50 to $100 until I could afford to do more. The key is not to wait for a ship to come in that you didn't send out. Start now with what you have and do something every month.

Another area I wanted to cover is leaving your job. Most employers offer some level of retirement account. If you or your employer have contributed to it, then when you leave your job, call your HR office and request that your retirement be transferred to another IRA even if it is a small one at your local bank. Once you no longer work at the company, it's important that you control your money versus assuming a company you no longer work for is taking care of your future. It's also important to know that when you start a new job and establish an IRA, your current bank IRA can be moved to your new plan and your new job.

There is hope even if you are approaching retirement

age. Although most people consider sixty-five retirement age, take the story of Colonel Harland Sanders. When he started his successful Kentucky Fried Chicken business, he was sixty-five-years old and living on a fixed income of a few-hundred dollars a month. Colonel Sanders died a rich man because he made his vision a reality.[6]

How well you enjoy your golden years depends upon how much you have saved for them. Social Security alone is not an adequate income for the average American. If you are of sound mind and in good health, it is never too late to begin working on a vision and making your dreams come true.

It is okay to treat yourself in the here and now if your finances are in order. Until then, you need to live within your means and prepare for your future. You have already taken the first step by using this book as a guide to help you get your finances under control.

3. Living Paycheck to Paycheck

According to financial expert Rebecca Lake, it is estimated that thirty-eight million USA households live from hand to mouth (that's old school for living paycheck to paycheck)—they spend every penny from every paycheck. Furthermore, twenty-six percent of Americans have no savings to fall back on in an emergency. Even more surprising is that 7.7 percent of adults do not have a bank account of any kind, either checking or savings.[7] These facts reveal a broken attitude toward money and savings. Fundamentally, with stabilizing your finances, it's not about what you make, it's about what you keep.

The fact is if you raise your level of spending every time you get a raise, you are still keeping yourself stuck in the same pattern of living from paycheck to paycheck. When you get a raise, rather than looking at it as having more money to spend, look at it as an opportunity to rework your budget. The percentages that go to necessities, bills, entertainment, and investments/savings shouldn't change. For example, if you budget to save fifteen percent of your income, then continue to save that much when you get a raise—that means you'll be saving *more*.

However, a raise may also be a good time to evaluate if you can increase the percentage you are putting into savings. For example, say you initially put five percent in savings because that was doable when you first started budgeting. Well, when you get a raise, consider upping the amount to ten percent even if that means you don't get to put any extra money toward entertainment. Ultimately, the size of your paycheck doesn't matter; living paycheck to paycheck without saving anything is a bad habit that does not build wealth.

This isn't what God intends or the Bible teaches. You can bring your finances in order by setting up a simple budget. Start by tracking your spending for one month. Record every penny you spend in a small notebook. This will allow you to see your actual spending pattern.

Dave Ramsey is one of the greatest authorities on finances and stewardship. He has an amazing free app called EveryDollar, which is a detailed budgeting tool.[8] All you have to do is plug your numbers into the categories and you are on your way. I also appreciate that Dave gives us a percentage of how much of our overall check we should be spending in each category. If you are married, the EveryDollar tool has the benefit of allowing you and your spouse to download the same app and be on the same page with your finances.

Whether you record all spending on an app or in a notebook, you can identify your unnecessary spending and remove it. After you do, then set up a monthly budget for yourself. Discipline yourself not to spend more than you have allotted for each category.

One of the most important things you can do is take a percentage of your earnings, maybe ten percent or whatever percentage you decide, and apply it toward a savings account—particularly one that earns good monthly interest. To develop wealth, you need to invest, and you need to save a percentage of every check that comes into your household. Preferably this account should be some type of pre-tax investment account. We'll go into details about those kinds of accounts later in this book.

You should allocate money for savings, just like money for any other bill in your budget. If you need to lower your monthly payments further, try consolidating bills into fewer payments. If you stick to your budget and make a habit of saving, you will have more money to meet your needs.

4. Borrowing Money Until Payday

Payday loan companies are designed to exploit you and keep you in debt. Companies like this prey on the fact that many people don't have the discipline to wait. That lack of patience will cost you a lot down the road. Some will automatically approve you for $100 to $500 per paycheck if you have a checking account and direct deposit of your paycheck. Then they will give you the loan with interest rates and fees that only deplete your resources and increase their assets.

For example, if you take a loan out for $100, your repayment amount is about $125 to $135 on your loan. If you cannot make the payment when the money is due, the loan company will add another $25 to $35 in late fees. Then you owe $170 on a $100 loan. If you are already in financial debt, why would you dish out $70 on every $100 that you borrowed when you can use the money you pay interest and fees on to open a savings account?

Another example is a place like "Rent-A-Center" that charges $10 to $20 per week for renting something. It may seem like you are spending less, but the result is you pay double what it would be if you waited responsibly to save enough to buy the item.

This example may tell of my age, but I think it will be worth it. When I was growing up, my family sometimes put something on layaway. That's when the store kept your product, and you paid on it as you could with no interest. It was not a line of credit. And once it was paid for, you picked up the couch you'd been paying on for ten months. When I look back on that, I understand the benefit of that program because the store was only holding it for you. It was not a loan, and you didn't take home the product until you fully paid for it.

Here's the bottom line. If you are overspending, failing to prepare for your future, or just being careless about how you are handling your finances, you will never become debt-free. You must control your spending and stick to a budget to begin your journey to financial freedom.

Financial Advisors and Planners

Proverbs 15:22 teaches us, "Without consultation, plans are frustrated, but with many counselors they succeed."

If the Bible says many advisors are our source of victory, then that applies to our finances too. If you are living in financial frustration, you should consult a financial planner. A financial planner will help you plan, save, and invest your dollars in the correct way.

It's important to understand there is a difference between a financial advisor and a Certified Financial Planner (CFP). A financial advisor focuses on investment counseling, but CFPs focus on helping you create a plan to reach your financial goals, including reduction of debt and tax planning. Unlike financial advisors, most CFPs are not commission-based but charge an hourly fee to help design a plan for you. Some of them base their fees on your net worth. In other words, your fee will be matched to what you can afford.

CFPs focus on helping people build long-term wealth. Some financial planners are licensed to do fee-based planning, but they usually have a minimum amount of assets they will accept. Do not be discouraged. You will find those willing to make an exception if you are serious about building wealth.

You can go to www.fpanet.org and look for a Certified Financial Planner. If you're still not comfortable in your search, ask for referrals from people you know who are financially successful. But don't be afraid to get help.

Four Rivers Instead of One

Eden, the garden where God placed Adam and Eve before the fall, was a fruitful paradise watered by four rivers (Genesis 2:10). Likewise, with finances, it is hard to develop a personal paradise when you have only one revenue stream.

Having more than one income stream is important and can help build financial security, but it does not always mean you must have more than one job. It could be having a well-funded retirement that will eventually be one of several income streams you can enjoy later.

I believe in working hard, but I also think it's important we understand that having more than one job may not be the solution for everyone. For example, if you have a job making $40,000 a year and you get an extra job that produces $15,000 a year, but you still have the same poor money habits, then chances are you will not see the benefit of an extra job. Rather than using that extra money wisely, you are simply increasing the cost of your lifestyle. Extra income would serve you better if you put it toward a strong savings account.

I believe it is important to use your creativity. If God has called you to launch a business, then launch that business. Think big, but start small. Keep your day job while you're starting this new business.

Once your household develops more than one revenue river, no single person becomes responsible for your financial future. In other words, no one can become your source. And that's a powerful feeling.

This may be the reason many people are angry and bitter with their bosses. They have subconsciously made their bosses responsible for their financial future instead of relying on God and themselves. But at the end of the day, their financial circumstance is about their financial mismanagement, not about their boss.

The Issue Is Self-Control

Money management boils down to an issue of self-control. Self-control is one of the Fruits of the Spirit listed in Galatians 5:22–23. If you do not have self-control in managing your resources, then you will experience hardship, debt, and financial frustration—all of which can set your marriage and family up for failure.

We will spend the rest of this book helping you get out of debt and build a strong financial future.

WORKBOOK

Chapter One Questions

Question: What are your current greatest financial challenges? What decisions and circumstances have led to these challenges? How has your financial situation negatively or positively impacted your marriage or your ability to get married at this time?

_____

_____

_____

_____

_____

_____

_____

_____

_____

_____

_____

Question: With your money habits are you wasting, spending, or investing? In what ways, good or bad, do your financial habits reflect your character—selfish or generous, proud or humble, impulsive or self-controlled? Are you patient in waiting for blessings in your life or do you struggle with delayed gratification?

_____

_____

_____

_____

_____

_____

_____

_____

_____

_____

Question: Which of these four—overspending, failing to prepare for your future, living paycheck to paycheck, or borrowing money until payday—most closely describes your current financial management? What hard choices do you need to make to break your bad habits and work toward financial freedom?

_____
_____
_____
_____
_____
_____
_____
_____
_____
_____

Take Action: Research different options for consulting with a financial planner. Talk to your pastor—some churches can recommend a church member or local Christian agency that can assist in working out of a financial hardship and meeting financial goals.

Take Action: Keep a detailed account of every expenditure in a small notebook (or use a budgeting program or app, whatever you will be most consistent to do). If you are in a relationship, both of you need to do this. Look for trends. How much are you spending on needs versus wants? Are there need areas (such as food and clothing) where you could reduce expenses by making more frugal choices?

Take Action: Brainstorm (with your spouse if you are married or your fiancé/fiancée if you are engaged) about additional rivers of income you could tap into to increase your ability to become financially secure.

Chapter One Notes

CHAPTER TWO

Money, Marriage, and Financial Stability

The first step to financial stability is comfortably providing for your immediate family. Disagreement over money has been cited among the top five reasons for divorce in America.[9] When marriages go through strife and difficulty, the source of the strife is often financial disagreements. If we can bring stability to our finances, there's a good chance we will bring stability to our marriages and families or future families. Because God cares so much about this, the Bible outlines many principles for handling our finances.

No Family Stability Without Financial Security

When you're broke, you're stressed. You can quote Psalm 23:1 all day long, "The LORD is my shepherd, I shall not want," but if you're broke, there's a lot of stuff you want. Peace is easier to maintain if you have something in your pocket, and your needs are provided for.

You can't tell God about your bills and ask Him to provide if you are irresponsible in your spending. Yes, God will meet your needs, but He is not obligated to your greed. He didn't approve of you buying that fancy coat or that holiday in the Bahamas when you couldn't afford it.

The best thing any couple can do is live within their means. In the early years of my marriage, our budget was very tight. I had broke-phobia. We had to learn the key to stewardship was having the money and not spending it. Just because the money comes in doesn't mean you need to send it out again immediately. Some people won't even save their tax refund. As we discussed in the previous chapter, immediately spending the entirety of the money you have will hinder your ability to develop wealth.

When I was in the storefront church, I would bring my little check to the bank every Friday. Every week, I'd tell the clerk I wanted twenty percent of it in the savings account, sixty percent of it in the checking account, and twenty percent of it in my wallet. At the time, my check was only $250, so $50 went into savings, $150 into checking, and $50 into my wallet.

I believe it's impossible to be spiritually free when you are financially bound. When I say financially bound, I mean the oppression that comes from living beyond your means. When you are trying to live bigger than your income—and you are plagued with debt and unnecessary bills—you are a slave to those lenders (Proverbs 22:7). Something weighs down your soul when every dime that comes in is obligated to somebody or something else.

That's not the abundant life Jesus came to give us (John 10:10). You do not have to be rich to be financially free, but you have to make wise decisions. This may mean living smaller—e.g., having a smaller home, buying clothes from a thrift store, and going without cable or streaming services. You may not have much, but at least you are free.

Men, It Starts with You!

The book of Proverbs, which is filled with the wisdom of Solomon, provides excellent tools for Christian men being molded into future husbands who provide for their families.

Proverbs 5:18 says, "Let your fountain be blessed, and may you rejoice in the wife of your youth." Throughout the book of Proverbs, Solomon gives us incredible advice on life before and during a marriage. Proverbs 5 provides a pattern for us to follow family and future family stability.

The wisdom espoused in Proverbs prepares any man for the woman described in the last chapter of this book as the *excellent wife*. This woman in Proverbs 31:10–25 is an ideal example of how a wife contributes to her household:

> *An excellent wife [other translations say "virtuous"], who can find? For her worth is far above jewels. The heart of her husband trusts in her, and he will have no lack of gain. She does him good and not evil all the days of her life. She looks for wool and flax and works with her hands in delight. She is like merchant ships; she brings her food from afar. She rises also while it is still night and gives food to her household and portions to her maidens.*

> *She considers a field and buys it; from her earnings she plants a vineyard. She girds herself with strength and makes her arms strong. She senses that her gain is good; her lamp does not go out at night. She stretches out her hands to the distaff, and her hands grasp the spindle. She extends her hand to the poor, and she stretches out her hands to the needy.*
>
> *She is not afraid of the snow for her household, for all her household are clothed with scarlet. She makes coverings for herself; her clothing is fine linen and purple. Her husband is known in the gates when he sits among the elders of the land. She makes linen garments and sells them, and supplies belts to the tradesmen. Strength and dignity are her clothing, and she smiles at the future.*

Although the excellent wife is helping sustain the household by being a caretaker and contributing toward the expenses, she's an extension of her husband. Financial health is a family effort. It isn't trying to balance the conflicting desires of the spender and the saver. Instead, it has to be a team goal. Each person might bring his or her unique personalities and habits to the table, but they need to be united in the goal of financial health and in making that reality happen.

First Timothy 3:5 states that if a man desires to be a leader in the church (a bishop or an elder), he is expected to have certain qualifications and characteristics for that position. According to this passage, a husband is called to take care of his household, "But if a man does not know how to manage his own household, how will he take care of the church of God?" This includes helping manage the finances wisely.

Paul further warns in 1 Timothy 5:8, "But if anyone

does not provide for his own, and especially for those of his household, he has denied the faith, and is worse than an unbeliever." Too many men today are ignoring their God-given responsibilities. How many of you know a thirty-something guy who has a dead-end, low-paying job, still lives with his mom, and gets his kids on the weekends but leaves them with his mom so he can go hang out with his friends? Men, that is not the person God wants you to be.

The Excellent Wife Shouldn't Marry a Deadbeat Guy

Women and families need financial security. As a man, you must know how to handle your finances before you get married because when you ensure your house is financially stable, it brings a certain comfort level to your spouse and family. In my church, I will not consent to marry a couple if the man is unemployed. I don't want to endorse a marriage like that.

I have seen many relationships where the woman pays for everything and thinks that's the way it's supposed to be. She's thanking the Lord for His goodness. The Lord is good, but if she's supporting the man, that's not the man she should marry. When God created Adam, the first thing he gave him before a woman was a job, "Then the LORD God took the man and put him into the garden of Eden to cultivate it and keep it" (Genesis 2:15).

After God created the world, He created man, placed him in a garden and told him to work the land, cultivate it, and let it produce. This means God never intended for work to be a curse; He meant it to be a blessing. Therefore, a man who chooses not to work is a curse to his family, and a man who chooses to work as God wants him to, is a blessing to his family.

I believe God has gifted our women to be just as successful as men, and successful women are all over the world. However, according to the Bible, it is still the man's responsibility to provide for his household. Ideally, a two-income family ought to live off of one income, while saving the other income. Can you imagine what life would be like if you saved the other income? Can you imagine what your retirement fund could look like? What about your children's college fund or your savings account? It is possible to be prosperous, but you must learn how to work with what you have and live below your means.

There is nothing wrong with a high-earning woman. But her income should supplement what her husband is making. At the same time, I do not think it is God's will for you to have multiple jobs to keep the bills paid. If you have to do that, then you need to reevaluate your spending and stick to a reasonable budget.

The Virtuous Woman

The word *virtuous* means someone of moral excellence or moral character.[10] This is one of the most important qualities of a good marriage. In the church, when you talk about a virtuous woman, everyone thinks you're talking about a spiritual woman. Yes, she is spiritual, but a virtuous woman is also a balanced woman. She is not just a woman who knows how to operate spiritually; she is a woman who knows how to operate practically. As we saw before, Proverbs 31 gives us the characteristics of a godly woman. The words of that chapter not only set the standard for what a woman should aspire to be, but it also shows what a man should look for in a woman.

One thing it shows is that her capabilities, interests, and hobbies far exceed her domestic abilities. In other words, a woman is comprised of so much more than her ability to wash dishes. This is a woman who understands how to make and save money and is cautious about spending it. She knows how to minister in the church and be around the things of God. She knows how to take care of her family. As a result, she is a balanced woman, and she is blessed.

A virtuous woman is trustworthy. Proverbs 31:11 states, "The heart of her husband trusts in her, and he will have no lack of gain." Every relationship, whether it is a dating or marriage relationship, has to have three things to be healthy: truth, trust, and transparency. Whenever you violate one, you violate the others. Even when a person messes up but comes back and asks for forgiveness, forgiveness is not equivalent to the restoration of trust.

A virtuous woman is a giver. Proverbs 31:20b says, "And she stretches out her hands to the needy." She is a woman who understands she is blessed to be a blessing (Genesis 12:2). Unfortunately, some people in the church do not think like this because most of them are more "need minded than seed minded."[11] Many women yearn to possess the qualities of the virtuous woman, but are unwilling to be generous. You must plant seeds. The Bible says, "By your standard of measure it will be measured to you in return" (Luke 6:38b).

It makes no difference what Wall Street is doing. God has an economic system Wall Street doesn't know about. God never loses investments; when you invest in the kingdom, it comes back. Luke 6:38a states, "They will pour into your lap a good measure—pressed down, shaken together, and running over." The size of your crop—the amount of seed you get into the ground—determines the size of your harvest. A virtuous woman is a giver regardless of the size of her income.

Another quality of the virtuous woman is she uses her gifts and abilities to contribute to her family. "She makes coverings for herself; her clothing is fine linen and purple" (Proverbs 31:22). Sometimes people earn an income with their creativity. Some people find a niche—they find a need and build on that until it grows into something larger. That's what the virtuous woman does. Although her husband is working and provides for his family, the virtuous woman still wants to contribute to their household.

Lastly, the virtuous woman is confident about the future. Proverbs 31:25 says, "Strength and dignity are her clothing, and she smiles at the future." The only way you can smile at the future is when you are prepared for it. Life was not meant to be lived in hopelessness with constant feelings of discouragement and defeat. The virtuous woman helps make this a reality for her family.

A Man of Integrity

Being virtuous is important for husbands, as well.

Proverbs 31 not only describes this extraordinary woman, but it tells us of the kind of man she is married to.

He is to be a man of honor. Verse 23 describes him as a man respected at the city gate, where he takes his seat among the elders of the land. The fact that he is sitting among the elders implies he is of good repute and in a position of higher authority. She is married to a good man who is working a good job and knows how to provide for his home.

He is to be a man of love. In Ephesians 5:31–33, the apostle Paul speaks of marriage by relating it to Christ and the church. Paul says a husband ought to love and cherish his wife in the same way he loves himself.

He is to provide for his family. Scripture teaches that when a husband leaves his parents' house, he is to take a bride, marry her, and the two become one flesh. He then has headship over the wife and home and is expected to provide for his family (Genesis 2:24, Ephesians 5:23, 1 Timothy 5:8).

As you can see, the Bible shows us the basics of establishing a Christian marriage.

Proverbs 31:10 says an excellent wife or a virtuous woman is worth far more than jewels. Men, pay close attention to this because here God describes the value of a godly woman. Think about the largest ruby in the world, maybe one that has yet to be discovered. How much money would something like that cost? Whatever the value is, the Bible says a virtuous woman—one of character and integrity, a woman who can be trusted with your life and resources—is worth more than that.

Now suppose you could buy that ruby and set it into a

ring for your virtuous woman. The next thing you must do is get it insured. Then, you probably will get a safe in the house to hold the ring when she does not wear it. You will do everything you can to protect that ring because you see it as valuable.

As valuable as that ruby ring is, God says a good woman is worth even more. If you treat that ring better than you treat the one wearing the ring, that's a problem. When you have a virtuous woman, you must treat her well.

One wise saying from Solomon in Proverbs 10:9 is, "He who walks in integrity walks securely." The man of integrity should want to make sure that if something happens to him, his family will have the provisions they need to survive.

If you want to be a man of integrity, you should leave an inheritance for your children and your children's children. Here are a few things you should do for your family:

1. Make sure you have enough life insurance, not only to cover your funeral expenses but also your mortgage and any debts your family may face when you are gone.

2. Have provisions for the cost of your children's college education.

3. Purchase disability insurance. Get a plan separate from your job's plan because you'll want more than a few months' worth of coverage. With disability insurance, most people never get enough coverage. They do not see it as

important. But if you are in your late thirties or forties, you should want to get enough disability insurance that will give you at least seventy percent of your take-home income. It is an investment worth the cost should you become injured or sick and cannot work.

Have the Hard Conversations

I do not believe you should marry someone who does not know how to handle money well. Each person in a marriage must trust that the other person can manage the money well. If there is a trust issue about money, that is a huge indicator you are not ready for marriage. Each marriage partner should be able to trust that the other will do the right thing with the money without supervision. If you lack trust during the engagement phase, you are entering your marriage with a severe division. If this division does not get resolved before marriage, it will only grow larger.

If you want to marry someone and one or both of you aren't good with money, you need to learn before you get married. Not everyone has grown up in a situation that has allowed them to learn how to handle their finances, but the key is they are *willing to learn* and do better. You and your potential spouse may even consider taking a financial stewardship class (preferably one recommended by your pastor) in conjunction with your premarital counseling. Having accountability in the process will enable you to discover blind spots and ensure you address the issue sufficiently before entering into marriage.

You might think that because you're getting paid, you don't have to worry about what your future spouse is making. But if you marry someone who cannot handle money, you will become one flesh with that person, and their bad financial habits will affect you. In other words, whatever dysfunction dwells in your future spouse's financial life will eventually be your problem too. As stated in Chapter One, whether you waste it, spend it, or invest it, what you do with your money is an indicator of what you do with your life.

You should know the money habits of your future spouse. One of you could be a spender and the other a saver. Or both of you could be spenders. If both of you are savers, you might think it is a perfect match. Not necessarily! With two savers, there may be a power struggle. Whatever your personal situation, you should discuss with your future spouse how you plan to operate financially in the long-term. How will you manage this money, and what responsibilities will each person take on?

Regardless of how you handle your money, both marriage partners should know what is going on with the finances. If you were to ask me who should be in charge of handling the money in the family, my answer would be whoever handles it best. Whoever is the most organized, the most disciplined, and the better steward over his or her finances ought to be the one.

Ideally, financial responsibility should be shared. For instance, one spouse could financially plan the first six months, and the other spouse could plan the next six months, and so on. Each spouse should have a say in the budget and the financial goals, and each spouse should hold the other accountable for big purchases and spending decisions. A lot of women make more money than their husbands, so it would be inconsiderate for that woman not to play a major role in the financial planning of that family.

It is the responsibility of both partners to understand the family finances. When both partners are involved, it relieves the stress that the spouse in charge of handling the money may be feeling. Knowing you are not alone makes the work a lot easier. And if a partner dies, the other ought to know where every dime is—the name of the bank, the account numbers, and whatever systems were being used to process the money.

Women, if you are thinking about getting married and your boyfriend or fiancé does not think like this or cannot discuss finances with you at this level, then he is not ready to be a husband. You should spare yourself time and pain, move on, and wait for God to place a faithful man into your life.

These are five worst-case scenarios I think are crucial to talk about in premarital counseling. These five things will help you understand where your partner's financial priorities lie and where your disagreements might be, and your expectations might differ:

1. One of you suddenly loses a job or source of income you've been relying on.
2. Your unemployment and/or severance pay is running out, leaving you without income.
3. You become disabled and must live on a

limited income.

4. The sudden loss of a spouse leaving your household with no income or one income instead of two.

5. There is an unexpected pregnancy, or a baby is born with a birth defect that requires long-term medical care. Or a relative, especially an elderly parent, becomes sick and needs financial help.

Addressing these types of hardships in detail in pre-marital counseling is critical. Planning for your financial future is one key to having a successful marriage.

Build Your House on the Rock

When Jesus fed the five thousand (Matthew 14:15–21), He put a process in place. He took the two fish and the five loaves—He broke them, He blessed them, and then He gave them out to feed a multitude. But before He did that, He said something significant to the crowd. He told them to sit down on the grass! Jesus was about to perform a miracle, but He was going to do it in an orderly fashion.

This suggests that before something great happens, there must be order. If there is no order, there can be no increase. This means a second step to financial stability is organization.

Jesus told a parable about the man who built his house on a rock and the man who built his house on the sand (Matthew 7:24–27). Now there is a common denominator in both scenarios. The storm hit both houses; however, the house that kept the family together was the one with a solid foundation on the rock and could stand against the storm.

In Luke 14:27–31, Jesus described builders who counted the cost before construction. While Jesus used this parable to challenge people to count the cost of following Him, it also tells us the importance of preparation and how the lack of it will keep you from completing what God has called you to do. You don't have to worry about tomorrow when you are prepared for it.

Believe it or not, some people do not think they will have a future, so they try to do everything right now. I believe if you work with what you have, you can get wherever you want to be in life.

How often have you heard someone say they need a raise or a job that pays more? However, often it's not about the raise, but about how they handle their finances. As I pointed out in Chapter One, you shouldn't raise your level of spending every time you get an increase in income. It is possible to live from paycheck to paycheck regardless of the size of the check.

How many times have we read about professional athletes who had millions of dollars but retire broke? They retired practically penniless because they believed the money would last forever. They didn't think their careers could come to a sudden or unexpected end. They got caught up in the cycle of big earning and big spending. This does not happen to all athletes or celebrities, but for those who get caught up in it, they have nothing to show for it in the end.

In his book *The Millionaire Mind*, Thomas Stanley surveyed 733 millionaires in the United States. He chronicled all the things he believed contributed to the success of the millionaires. The results were quite interesting. Below is a summary of some factors they said contributed to their success:[12]

1. Being honest with all people. In other words, walking in integrity.
2. Being well-disciplined. You've got to be well-disciplined to be successful at anything in life.
3. Having a supportive spouse. Ninety percent of them had been married to the same spouse for over twenty-five years.
4. Working harder than most people are willing to work.
5. Loving their careers.
6. Living beneath their means. I think this is an interesting fact. The majority of those interviewed lived in houses that cost half-a-million dollars or less.

These are all principles we can take to heart as we think about the future of our families.

Part of providing for our family is providing for our family's future. When you have a plan, God will get involved in it, "Commit your works to the LORD and your plans will be established" (Proverbs 16:3).

In everything God does, even though He has all power,

He still has a plan. He had a plan to rectify sin when Adam and Eve sinned. His son Jesus would be the Lamb without spot, wrinkle, or blemish who would come and die for our sins (John 1:29). Three days later, He would rise from the grave (Luke 24:1–8). He had forty days of post-resurrection ministry; then, He ascended back to the Father (Acts 1:1–3). God has a plan that one day Jesus will come back (Hebrews 9:28).

He has all the capability of doing whatever He wants to do. He can say, "Let there be light" (Genesis 1:3), and light shows up! He's got that much power. But for God to have that much power and still have a plan must mean that planning is an important part of His design.

Dare To Dream for the Future

We all have goals for our futures and families. Wouldn't it be great if—through careful planning, responsible living, and trust in God—those dreams came true? What are your goals? Your dreams? As for me, I want to live my latter years doing the work of the ministry, reaching our community, and enjoying my children as they grow into adulthood. If you prepare for your future, you'll have options when you get there.

People in poverty and lack will always be under the authority of those making the decisions. Proverbs 22:7 says, "The rich rules over the poor." When you are struggling financially, you don't have as many options, and those with more money and power may be positioned to dictate the direction of certain aspects of your life. However, when you are financially secure because you have planned, you're empowered to create your options and opportunities, instead of money dictating it for you.

Think about it—when you have grandchildren, wouldn't it be awesome to help them pay for their first year of college because you have paid off your house and cars and have nothing but utilities and taxes to pay on the house? That would not only encourage the grandkids, but it would also teach them sound financial habits. That kind of blessing doesn't come without careful and responsible financial planning. You may just be starting your family, but if you follow the principles in this book, you can get to that point.

Hopefully, the points in this chapter have helped you, think about the kind of spouse you want to marry and the kind of spouse you want to be. These principles will help you to be financially successful in your marriage. If you're already married, I hope this chapter has been helpful to set you on your journey to financial success in the future. In the following chapters, we will discuss in more detail how to get out of debt, build a financial future, and maintain financial freedom.

WORKBOOK

Chapter Two Questions

Question: *For men:* How are you living out the mandate to be a leader of integrity? Are you taking responsibility for your family's financial security (or future family if you are not married)? Can you supply adequate income for the household so that your wife's income is supplemental or can be put into savings? If you are married, are you treasuring your wife as more precious than costly jewels, and how do you show her that you value her?

_____

_____

_____

_____

_____

_____

Question: *For women:* Are you modeling the Virtuous Woman in looking for creative ways to supplement your family's income? Does (or will) your husband trust you to wisely manage the income he provides? What are some creative ways you can live the life you want within your means or that you can adjust your expectations to fit within what your husband can provide? How are you generous toward those in need? How can you become confident about your family's future?

Question: If you are in a relationship, discuss with your spouse or fiancé (fiancée) the five "worst-case scenarios." Are you prepared for any of them? How? Which ones are you unprepared for, and what needs to change to have a plan in place in case any of these life events catches you by surprise? Review your life insurance and disability insurance plans and be sure they are adequate for your current and future needs.

_____
_____
_____
_____
_____
_____
_____
_____
_____
_____

Take Action: Begin reading through the book of Proverbs. You can read one chapter a day that corresponds with that day of the month, and you will finish in a month. Write down or note all verses that have to do with money and financial responsibility, as well as verses about marriage and the role of a husband/wife. Commit these verses to memory and look for ways to apply this practical wisdom to your life.

Take Action: If you are not married, make a list of the financial goals you personally need to meet before you are ready to take on the responsibility of marriage. Also, write out what you expect from your future spouse in terms of their financial management and money management principles. How will you ensure that you trust each other and are in agreement about your finances before you get married?

Take Action: What are some ways God is a God of order? How do you see God working by a plan? Would you say your finances are orderly and well-planned or haphazard? Dream about how you would like to live and how you could give by achieving financial freedom. From these dreams, write tangible goals, and then prayerfully work through a plan to bring your finances into order and achieve your goals.

Chapter Two Notes

CHAPTER THREE

Dealing with Debt

Putting your faith in God isn't passive—it's a choice to live right. When you decide you want to live right and give your life to Christ, blessings come. With those blessings come wisdom over the situations in your life, and God teaches you discernment and how to be shrewd in your thinking.

In Chapter One, I said it is impossible to gain control over your life if you can't gain control over your finances. We may long for eternity with God, but for now, we live on Earth. We have to work, pay bills, and provide for our loved ones. Debt makes it harder to do these things. Just like you can't pray to God and sit back and hope everything works out, you can't ignore debt and just hope it goes away. You must have strategies and a plan to get out of debt.

I have received some powerful testimonies from various members of my congregation who have implemented the principles in this book for stewarding their finances.

Members have shared that their salaries have doubled, and they have seen God do amazing things in their life as a result of improving their stewardship. I've received emails, cards, and letters sharing that they have dramatically reduced the debt they owe and have seen their finances improve.

These things are possible when we follow God's principles for our financial stewardship. I want you to grab hold of this and believe God with me that you can trust Him for great things. When we listen to the wisdom and guidance of God for handling our finances, opportunities open to us! But, as I mentioned previously, we need to have a plan for that increase rather than merely increasing our spending.

In this chapter, I want to deal with debt. It is time for you to handle this stronghold that holds so many people in bondage. You can't get out of debt if you don't deal with it and face it head-on. You cannot try to escape it by ignoring it because it will catch up with you. If you do not make tough decisions regarding your debt, your debt will make those decisions for you.

Wisdom to Get Out of Debt

Wisdom is defined as "the ability to judge correctly and follow the best course of action based on your knowledge and understanding."[13] In other words, wisdom comes when you base your decisions on the information you gather before the decision. If you lack wisdom, the Bible says the source of wisdom is God. When you seek God for wisdom, He will give you wisdom. James 1:5 states,

"But if any of you lacks wisdom, let him ask of God, who gives to all generously and without reproach, and it will be given to him."

Dr. Ed Cole, known as the father of the Christian Men's Movement, defines it this way, "God's pattern for victory is: wisdom, strategy, victory. Men want victory; God gives strategy."[14] While his ministry is geared toward men, this truth is relevant for men and women alike. Wisdom gives a strategy for victory that results in glory. A lot of believers never experience the glory of God because they lack wisdom, and if they lack wisdom, they don't have a strategy. If they don't have a strategy, they can't achieve victory.

We don't hear many sermons in the church that help us understand the Bible's principles on money. As a result, believers with a vision lack the wisdom and resources to finance that vision. When they don't have the right wisdom and resources, they are more likely to make financial mistakes and get into debt. Thankfully, God has given us His Word with plenty of wisdom to help us make good financial decisions, and we can trust what He says about money.

Why Are You in Debt?

Have you asked yourself what caused you to be in debt? What do you think has caused you to struggle for so long financially? Every person's situation is unique, but I think a common problem is Christians praying God's promises but violating God's principles. In other words, you understand the promises of God, and you stand on those promises because the promises are true. However, you forget that those promises are dependent on the principles.

If you claim the promises but violate the principles, you will never get the blessings. A lot of Christians have been praying for a long time and wonder why God has not given them their harvest. One reason could be that Christians are continuously violating one of God's principles in money management by living paycheck to paycheck. To get a harvest, you have to qualify for the harvest by showing God you can be trusted with His provisions.

We see this bad habit of living paycheck to paycheck played out in our culture all the time. Recently, the state of New Jersey was hit with a budget crisis, and the government shut down all government agencies and major businesses. This has also happened in other parts of our country. The government provided over half of the jobs in the state. The news stations interviewed workers who were jobless during those few days. The people talked about the pressure and issues this shutdown caused for their families.

The number of people in this country who file for bankruptcy is hard to believe. I am not judging anyone as it relates to bankruptcy, I'm simply saying bankruptcy is only part of the problem because the bankruptcy does not address the issue that got you into that position. It reveals a character problem that plagues our culture. Here are some common reasons so many fall into these financial hardships.

1. We make ill-informed purchases.

We are lazy about doing our homework before we make a big purchase, like a car. Consider this scenario: a salesperson at a dealership approaches you and asks, "How much can you afford to pay?" I would advise you to never answer that question because they are asking about how much you want to pay monthly. You should negotiate the price of the car, not the price of the monthly payment. They can stretch your car payments over five to six years. That is how car dealers get you to overpay for a vehicle.

To get the best price and interest rate for something like a car purchase, you should look in places like the *Kelley Blue Book* to find the real value of the car and explore other lending institutions. Go to that car dealer knowing what amount their banks will lend you if you finance the car through them. Then, if you are offered a higher interest rate, you can negotiate it down. It will show them you are an educated consumer, and better yet, will keep you within your budget.

2. We can only afford the minimum monthly payment.

Most people assume they are doing okay because they can afford the minimum monthly payments on a loan or credit card. When you have the mentality of just affording the minimum payment, you are not looking at the big picture. You ignore the amount of interest you will pay over the course of the loan. So the faster you pay off a loan, the less interest you owe a bank or other lender.

3. We wait too long before seeking help.

Do not be embarrassed to ask for help when you run into financial problems. Sometimes, you need professional advice when you need to gain control over your lifestyle. People will let their mortgage get four months behind before they acknowledge they are slipping into a financial crisis. However, these same people will approach members of their church, saying, "I need $7,000 by tomorrow."

If you have failed to ask for help early on, it's not the responsibility of others to bail you out when it becomes a crisis. Talk to a professional budget counselor who can help you set up a monthly payment plan and get you out of your crisis. Then, resolve to make better financial choices—as outlined in this book—in the future.

4. We misuse or overuse credit cards.

One major reason we get trapped in financial hardship is that we use credit cards as a survival tool instead of a convenience. If you cannot afford to pay off the entire amount at the end of every month, then you cannot afford to use your credit card. If you frequently abuse credit cards—that is, spending more with your credit card than you can pay off at the end of the month—make a habit of only paying with cash. If you cannot afford to pay for an item, save up until you have enough money to do so. It's that simple. Credit card debt is easily avoided, and yet it cripples the lives of so many people.

Credit Card Use and Abuse

Many people start accumulating credit card debt the minute they step onto a college campus. Not only are many new college students taking on student loans, but often within the first few weeks of college, credit card companies set up booths in student unions and try to sign kids up for them early. If you don't teach your child about biblical economics, they'll think your credit card is magic, and all they have to do is get old enough to have one themselves. Many of these young adults can't handle them, and it'll set them up for a precarious financial future.

They're not credit cards; they're debt cards. The label is misleading. They don't give you credit; they give you debt. For many people in our culture, credit cards are nothing more than a self-imposed payday loan. They use it between checks. The danger of doing this is you get the item you want, but you get a bill later.

You should be able to entirely pay off a credit card at the end of the month. You can't treat it like a magic card and keep making purchases without considering that you're obligated to pay that off in thirty days. If you don't, you've essentially stolen those items, and you're now in debt with interest on top of what you owed for the goods. You've got to pay stuff down if you don't want to be in a huge financial hole.

Credit cards aren't evil in themselves, but the card should work for you—you shouldn't work for it. Some people have the discipline to use them and do all the time. However, my concern is when it gets out of control. The power of paying cash is you tend to spend less than when you use credit. And you can enjoy the purchase with a sense of peace because you don't have to stress over new bills you created.

If you're going to get your money straight, you've got to have a financial IQ and be willing to honestly face how much debt you have. Remember, it's not sinful to have debt; it's sinful to have too much debt—and that has more to do with what the debt reveals about your heart and character rather than the debt itself. People with too much debt are broke, and if you're working on getting out of debt, you can expect a "broke" season as you straighten your finances and reorient your priorities.

If you humble yourself, then that broke season will teach you some important lessons. You'll be forced to get creative in meal preparation, you'll learn to buy store brands instead of name brands, you'll cut coupons, and you may not darken the door of restaurant or movie theaters for several months. It'll take a radical change in lifestyle.

When you look at debt like this, honestly and radically, you'll change the way you approach money. There's no stress when what you own is paid for. And that's the point we all want to get to. In the next section, we'll look at specific ways you can get out of debt as quickly as possible.

Debt Is a Slave Master

When you are in debt, the Bible says you are enslaved to your creditors. "The rich rules over the poor, and the borrower becomes the lender's slave" (Proverbs 22:7).

When you continue to borrow, it enslaves you! It is hard to enjoy something you buy on credit when you are in bondage to a lender.

Ecclesiastes 5:10a says, "He who loves money will not be satisfied with money, nor he who loves abundance with its income." It's important to distinguish between desire and love. There is nothing wrong with desiring money, but being in love with money is the problem. The apostle Paul further explained, "For the love of money is a root of all sorts of evil, and some by longing for it have wandered away from the faith and pierced themselves with many griefs" (1 Timothy 6:10).

If you are in love with money, you will never be satisfied with your salary. If you are in love with money, you will make bad decisions to get more money and more stuff. It may even cause you to lead yourself and your family away from the Lord.

At some point, you have to choose to either live your life discontent with your job, your salary, your stuff, and your relationships, or you can resolve to be content and appreciative of the blessings God has already given you until you can change your situation.

If you refuse to be content with what God has already blessed you with, you will end up living life bitter and resentful and envious of others. You will be more likely to make bad financial decisions that will affect you and your family negatively. The benefit of being content is you can have peace on the way to your goal of purchasing items you desire.

Regardless of your financial status, I think it's important that you understand happiness is not a location.

Stop saying, "I'll be happy when I'm eighteen, or when I finish college, or when I'm married, or when I'm making six figures." God wants you to learn how to enjoy the journey on the way to your destination.

In Matthew 18:23–35, Jesus told a parable about a slave who owed his master a huge debt. While this parable is ultimately about forgiveness, it contains insight into the severity of debt. This slave owed ten-thousand talents, which nowadays is equal to approximately two-million dollars. Verse 25 says, "But since he did not have the means to repay, his lord commanded him to be sold, along with his wife and children and all that he had, and repayment to be made."

Do you see what that does to a family? Debt enslaves you. It can cause you to lose your marriage and family. Creditors can repossess items you have accumulated.

Financial issues that do not get settled contribute to the demise of marriages which ultimately end in divorce. Dr. Edwin Louis Cole says that the place of agreement is the place of power.[15] In Acts 2, they were all together on one accord, and the power of God fell. When the devil attacks your relationship or your marriage, he always targets your agreement. I believe he does this because once you get the couple out of unity and agreement, the relationship loses its power and is at greater risk. Even when divorce comes, people end up paying attorneys thousands of dollars to fight over who gets the kids and who gets the money and property. Divorce doesn't always solve the problems with money; it often compounds them.

The rest of the parable describes the slave falling at his master's feet and begging him to give him time to pay off the debt. On his salary, it would take multiple lifetimes for him to pay off the debt. So, feeling compassion for his slave, the master forgave his debt. It was the only way he would be free of it.

The man in the parable did something responsible, though: he approached his creditor and asked for mercy in helping to pay off the debt. This showed good character and taught us how we should approach debt in our lives. Even when you don't have the money to pay the bill, you should call the company you owe ask, to speak to the billing department, and let them know why you may be late on your payment this month and that you fully plan to pay it. When creditors hear things like that, they are much more willing to work with the people until they are up to date on their bill. Maybe it was one reason the master had compassion on the slave and forgave his debt. We could call this "supernatural debt cancelation."

The parable then describes the slave approaching another man who owed him a much smaller amount of money. When that man couldn't pay back the slave, the slave threw him in prison until he could pay what he owed. The master found out about what the slave had done, called him back, and tortured him until he could pay off his debt. Here was a man who had been forgiven and blessed and was unwilling to be a blessing to somebody else.

At the end of this parable, Jesus challenged His disciples to bless others the same way that master blessed his slave and to not turn around and behave the way the slave did. If God has released you from your life's strongholds, is it too much for you to be a blessing to somebody else?

If you deal honestly with your debt, watch what God does. You may think it will take a long time to get out of debt, but if you exercise good character and have a desire to pay back what you owe, God steps into the middle of your situation and accelerates your deliverance. The unjust servant got the blessing. He approached it and dealt with it rightly, but then he committed an error in judgment when he was in the position of creditor instead of borrower. Let's not be that way with handling our finances.

The Six Dangerous Causes of Debt

Maybe you're reading this, and you don't think this applies to you because you're not in debt yet. Maybe you're thinking, "I could change some of my bad habits, but I'm not in debt yet, so what is there to worry about?" If you're not in debt yet, that's great, but read on to see if any of these dangerous causes of debt are accurate reflections of your situation and habits. If they are, it's time to make changes *now* before you find yourself in a financial crisis.

1. You live on credit instead of paying cash.

Relying on credit cards is a huge indicator you are spending beyond your means. In 2019, studies showed that people ages 35–44 had an average of $8,235 of credit card debt, people ages 45–54 had a whopping $9,096 of credit card debt, ages 55–64 had an average of $8,158 in credit card debt, and senior citizens, ages 70–74, had an average of $6,465 of credit card debt.[16] This is outrageous!

There are two main problems when people don't have the discipline to handle credit cards the right way. One, it shows a lack of contentment. I understand this. If I had the resources, I'd get four or five cars. I like cars! But everything you do has to be done in stages. A lack of contentment is the inability to wait until God brings you to a place where you can do it. Two, using credit presumes your future—you're spending money you don't actually have yet.

So how do you know if you're making the right purchase? By understanding your budget. It's not whether you can afford something, but whether you can afford it with money to spare. You shouldn't get a car if you're stressed about the payment at the end of every month. That's not abundant living.

2. You delay payments or only make the minimum payment.

If you are running out of money at the end of the month and unable to pay your bills, then that is a sign your finances are out of control. Also, as we said earlier, the longer you only make the minimum monthly payment on your credit card or loan, the more interest you will owe over time.

3. You are unable to tithe and save.

If all your money is going to bills, and you have nothing left over for your church or your savings, then you might be in danger of a financial crisis. If this is your situation, consider tithing and saving first before you pay any of your bills.

One thing I have found helpful is the 10/10/80 principle. When I get my paycheck, I pay God (my local church, charities) ten percent. I pay myself ten percent to set aside for savings, and then I pay for everything else out of the remaining eighty percent. Whatever we have left out of that, we work with. It's a sad thing when you can put in two weeks of exhausting work, and then you can't even be happy about getting your paycheck because somebody else already has a claim on all your money. There's something wrong with that. Saving and tithing help you see something worthwhile come out of all your labor, so you have to make those things a priority in your life.

4. You are unable to pay your taxes.

The Bible is clear—we are to obey the laws of the land and pay the government what we owe in taxes: "…render to Caesar the things that are Caesar's; and to God the things that are God's" (Matthew 22:21). Not paying your taxes will land you in all sorts of legal and financial trouble. If you're not saving enough to pay Uncle Sam, you're setting yourself up for a major financial crisis.

5. You spend extravagantly.

In Chapter One, we discussed overspending and how it reveals a lack of self-control. It also reveals we are not content with what God has given us. Overspending leads to the previous four danger signs: credit card debt, unable to pay your bills, a lack of ability to tithe and save for emergencies, and an inability to pay your taxes.

We need to be content with what God has given us. Personally, I haven't felt pressure to get something because somebody else has it, and I've been this way for twenty years. I'm not saying I'm perfect at all, but I know what it's like to struggle, to have two college degrees and a little storefront church, and to eat Hamburger Helper® every day in a small apartment. Anybody who's got something from God has been through something to get there, but it takes being content with the current situation before you can move onto the next one.

6. You're always looking for a "get-rich-quick" scheme.

If someone promises that you can make lots of money with little effort, then believe me, it's too good to be true. A lot of multi-level marketing companies are out there, and oftentimes they make big promises only to leave a person worse off financially. Some do a great job and have a good system, but it's up to you to ensure that any company you work for uses an ethical business model. I encourage you to do your homework on any job or venture you plan to go into to see how you might fit into it. I express this concern because I have seen so many people get involved in something before they really understood it, and it led to a myriad of problems. Doing your homework will also position you to be more effective in that company if you choose to work there.

Money is made through hard work and discipline on

your part, not on other's parts. Proverbs 13:11 says, "Wealth gained hastily will dwindle, but whoever gathers little by little will increase it" (ESV).

Break the Stronghold of Debt

You must decide to break the debt stronghold. It doesn't matter if you grew up in a family that lived from paycheck to paycheck, and you've continued that same pattern in your marriage and family. You must decide that is over, and your story will be different.

If you want financial stability, you have to understand knowledge is power. Ignorance makes us weak and susceptible to making bad decisions. One reason we are seeing a change in the lives of some believers is that over the last ten to fifteen years, ministers have taught more in the area of finances. I believe if we teach on it, and you use the knowledge we talk about, then the Spirit of God will release something into your situation that will change your life radically and permanently.

In addition to the topics covered in this chapter, it is also wise to educate yourself in the areas of your life that need to be changed. Read financial books, newspapers, and magazines. Familiarize yourself with financial terms and money management principles. Once you are comfortable with those, move up to financial books. Many financial books make learning about money management interesting. You must commit to educating yourself on how to handle your money.

Money is not supposed to control you—you're supposed to control money. If you are in the same financial hole you were in a year, or two years, or three years ago, then your situation must change now. It is choking you to where you feel there is no way out. Debt is a stronghold that can lead to mental ailments such as stress, which is known to cause hypertension and other physical problems. If you learn to take control of your money, you can reclaim your lifestyle and take a different approach to handle your finances.

You must develop a mentality of delayed gratification if you get control of your finances. Some people try to accumulate in three years what it took their parents thirty years to build up. You must learn to take each development as a step-by-step process, rather than try to have everything right away.

I also believe there is a psychology to debt. There is something about a person who has had that paycheck-to-paycheck mentality for so long that they think it's normal. That's a stronghold in your life, and it has caused you to develop an unbiblical mentality. It is unbiblical for you to live your life paycheck to paycheck. God not only desires to give you blessings, but He also wants to use you to be a blessing to others. You can't do that if you're stuck in debt.

We will spend the next chapter discussing specific ways you can get out of debt. As you continue to journey through this book, I pray this information will help answer some questions you were afraid to ask before. Maybe you felt embarrassed and did not want to seek help, thinking you were the only one in your situation and that no one would understand your problems.

I'm here to tell you God wants you to come out of this

lifestyle of slavery to debt. He loves you, and He knows you love Him. It may take time and hard work and making some tough choices, but you will free yourself of debt, and you will do it with God's help—who provides wisdom and knowledge. This book will enable you to reclaim the life God has planned for you while you were in your mother's womb (Jeremiah 1:5).

WORKBOOK

Chapter Three Questions

Question: Are you in debt? How much? What kind of debt? What factors, circumstances, and attitudes have contributed to your debt? Have you been living according to God's principles and believing His promises regarding your money?

_____

_____

_____

_____

_____

_____

_____

_____

Question: What are some ways you can do effective research and make wise decisions about necessary purchases to be sure you are balancing quality and cost? What are some items you could buy pre-owned rather than new? What are some items you could buy in an "off" brand rather than a brand name? How will you apply wisdom to when, what, where, and how you buy?

Question: Which of the six danger signs of debt do you see in your life? What are some practical steps you can take right away to stop accruing additional debt and to begin the process of becoming debt-free?

_____
_____
_____
_____
_____
_____
_____
_____
_____
_____
_____

Take Action: *If you refuse to be content with what God has already blessed you with, you will end up living life bitter and resentful and envious of others.* Make out a gratitude list of all the blessings—tangible and intangible—God has given you. Review this list when you are tempted to feel sorry for yourself because of what you don't have.

Take Action: How can you and your spouse or future spouse further educate yourselves on financial management? Ask your pastor or a wise Christian mentor to recommend books, magazines, workshops, etc. that will aid you in understanding and excelling at money management.

Take Action: Set aside a lunch hour to pray and fast about your financial situation. Ask God to deliver you from a spirit of poverty, from the stronghold of debt, and from greed and selfishness in your decisions. Pray for wisdom from the Holy Spirit and seek wisdom from God's Word for your financial future. Thank God for His love and provision in your life and ask for His grace and strength to make the right choices.

Chapter Three Notes

CHAPTER FOUR

Rapid Debt Reduction

In the last chapter, we discussed the biblical approach to avoiding and managing debt. In this chapter, I want to focus on ways to achieve rapid debt reduction and the strategies you can implement to change your financial future. When you are exercising good stewardship and financial discipline, God can accelerate the process of bringing you out of debt.

If you are not yet married, the time to get out of debt is now so that if and when God provides a spouse for you, you are well on your way to financial success and freedom. If you're married, getting out of debt will alleviate the stress surrounding finances in your family's life and ensure you and your kids have a prosperous future.

We Are a Nation in Debt

Credit card debt in the US is staggering. Again, the last thing I want to do is make someone feel condemned because you have debt. My goal is to see all of us eventually become debt-free. Not all my financial decisions have been good ones either. So if you feel overwhelmed because you're still trying to figure out how to pay off your debt, think about this. Illuminating it will take hard work, discipline, and a lot of time. But I believe the process of paying off your debts builds the character and discipline needed to maintain long-term healthy financial habits.

Debt in the Bible:
Elisha and the Widow's Oil

Debt is not a new problem, and in the Bible, being in debt often had much more serious consequences than it does today. Take the story of Elisha and the widow from 2 Kings 4:1–7:

> *Now a certain woman of the wives of the sons of the prophets cried out to Elisha, "Your servant my husband is dead, and you know that your servant feared the Lord; and the creditor has come to take my two children to be his slaves."*
>
> *Elisha said to her, "What shall I do for you? Tell me, what do you have in the house?"*
>
> *And she said, "Your maidservant has nothing in the house except a jar of oil."*
>
> *Then he said, "Go, borrow vessels at large for yourself from all your neighbors, even empty vessels; do not get a few. And you shall go in and shut the door behind you and your sons, and pour out into all these vessels, and you shall set aside what is full."*
>
> *So she went from him and shut the door behind her and her sons; they were bringing the vessels to her and she poured.*

When the vessels were full, she said to her son, "Bring me another vessel."

And he said to her, "There is not one vessel more." And the oil stopped. Then she came and told the man of God. And he said, "Go, sell the oil and pay your debt, and you and your sons can live on the rest."

The woman's husband was a prophet who served God but died leaving debts. Her sons were to be taken as slaves to pay the debt. In the present day, no one will take away your kids to pay off a debt, but in that culture and time, that was a real danger when someone was in debt. So the widow went to Elisha, the prophet—this man of God, the one chosen to succeed the prophet, Elijah—for help in her crisis.

According to verse 2, Elisha asked, "What shall I do for you?" Notice Elisha didn't get distracted with the emotions of debt. He was ready to be practical. In the same way, stop letting people emotionally manipulate you when they need money. Furthermore, with your debt, you have to think practically about the situation and what you can do to start getting out of it.

Elisha asked the widow, "Tell me, what do you have in your house?" Isn't it amazing that for most miracles, you've got to have something to start something? For instance, before Jesus fed the five thousand, a little boy had to give up his lunch. Elisha wanted to know what the widow had on hand to help her get out of debt. We cry out to God for a miracle but don't give Him anything. As long as you hold on to what you have, that's all you have. You need to learn to sow seeds out of your need. Even if you feel you have nothing to give, you must be willing to invest the resources you *do* have to get out of debt. There can be no harvest if you do not first plant the seed.[17]

"Your maidservant has nothing in the house except a jar of oil," she replied (2 Kings 4:2b). Oil was valuable in biblical times, so this was something Elisha could work with. He gave the widow a debt-elimination strategy, then made her an entrepreneur in the oil business.

"Go and borrow empty vessels," Elisha told her. She had one jar of oil, but he instructed her to get as many empty vessels as she could find. Sometimes faith doesn't make sense, but you need to trust that God is working and obey Him. The miracle happened when she poured oil from her one jar, and the empty vessels kept filling up. When there were no more vessels to fill, the oil ran out.

While they were filling the jars, Elisha told them to shut the door of their house (2 Kings 4:4). Sometimes God doesn't want the whole world to know your struggle. Not everybody in your life has to know your problem, especially those people who may make it harder for you to do the things God is calling you to do. Make sure your spouse and kids know what's going on, but beyond that, this is between you and God.

Notice her sons helped her with this—you need to involve everybody in your family to help you get out of debt. As we've discussed in previous chapters, you need to be on the same page with your spouse, and likewise, your kids need to understand your family's culture will be different while you do what's necessary to get out of debt. If you have one person working against you, it will be a lot harder to eliminate debt. Do whatever you can to get your family on board with your financial goals. Your family's financial situation affects everyone in the family. So while your kids may not work, they need to participate because it matters for their lives too. This will only work toward teaching them healthy financial habits as they grow.

Once all the oil jars were filled, Elisha gave the widow an economic strategy to get her out of debt—she was to sell the oil to pay off the debt. The amount of oil produced in the miracle must have been worth more than the debt, because Elisha further instructed, "You and your sons can live on the rest" (2 Kings 4:7). Elisha was essentially providing a retirement income for the widow. There was so much money left over that she could live off it for the rest of her life. Because she handled her resources God's way, she generated income to support herself. For a widow in biblical times, this was a big relief.

The Bible never stops being relevant to our lives. When we follow God's principles, He helps us solve our financial problems. He may even come through with a miracle you didn't expect. Later in the chapter, we'll discuss specific strategies to get out of debt as quickly as possible so you can live the way God wants you to live.

Six Steps to Rapid Debt Reduction

As a child of God, you have a responsibility to pay your bills. Romans 13:8 instructs, "Let no debt remain outstanding, except the continuing debt to love one another, for whoever loves others has fulfilled the law" (NIV). As Christians, when we can see our debt as a biblical issue and not a financial issue, we are more motivated to eliminate debt in our lives. With that in mind, here are six steps for reducing your debt quickly.

Step 1: Pay extra to lower bills. Figure out what your lowest debt or bill is, and then pay extra on that to lower your bill. For instance, if your lowest bill is $1,000 and has a monthly payment of $50, pay an extra $20 every payment. Now you're paying $70 per month toward a $50 monthly bill. Once that bill is paid off—and it will happen faster and with less interest, since you increased the payment—rather than using the $70 for something else, take that $70 and add it to what you are already paying on the next lowest bill.

When your second-lowest bill is paid off, take the $70-plus payment from the second-lowest bill and apply it to the next lowest debt and so forth. The debts will disappear more quickly, and you'll pay less in interest. That is rapid debt reduction.

Step 2: Pay extra on your mortgage once a year. If you have a mortgage, try to make an extra payment on it at least once a year. By doing this, you can cut years off your mortgage and pay off your house quicker.

Here are two ways you can do this:

1. Make biweekly payments on your mortgage. You have to make special arrangements with your mortgage company to do this, but if you can get on a program where you're paying a balance every two weeks, you will decrease the interest applied to the loan, and by the end of the year, you'll have made a full extra payment

on the house.

2. If you do not want to make biweekly payments, you can achieve the same goal by paying monthly as you normally would and writing an extra check at the end of the year.

Regardless of which you choose, you'll pay off your house faster and owe less interest to the bank. You can also use a similar process for paying off a car more quickly. Keep in mind; this is not initiated by your contract; this is something you do of your own initiative—you intentionally send the loan company an extra payment.

Step 3: Use your income tax refund to pay down debt. Your income tax refund is extra money and can help get you out of debt. Use part of your tax return toward debt and save part of your return too. For instance, if you get a $2,000 tax refund, use $1,500 to pay toward some bills, then save the rest. Building savings helps you not to fall short when you hit a financial emergency, like a medical bill or car repair.

Step 4: Transfer your credit card debt to a card with zero percent interest. Transfer your debt to a new credit card that gives you one year at Zero percent interest. This gives you twelve months of interest-free payments that go straight to the principal on that loan. This will enable you to pay off what you owe quickly.

Step 5: Continue to make payments to yourself after the last payment. This works especially well for car payments. Many people think they need a new car because their current one is old, and they're still making payments. Here's a better plan for purchasing the new car. Pay off the car you are currently driving, and once it is paid off, keep making payments on the car but make them to yourself into a savings account designated for your next car purchase. Continue driving the car you paid off "until the wheels are about to fall off."

If you can continue driving the old car that's paid off for two-and-a-half years, and you're saving what you would've made in a car payment, you will have two and a half years' worth of money in that account toward the purchase of your new car. You will also have the trade-in value of your old car. With this money, you no longer need five years to pay off the loan. You may be able to pay off that new car loan in two years.

Step 6: Downsize. Some of us are living in houses we cannot afford. If you cannot afford your current mortgage, if you're "house poor," downsize and sell the house before the bank forecloses on you. Do not wait until you are in a financial crisis or you will end up dodging bills and ruining your credit for the next several years. Use wisdom. It is possible to find a smaller house at a good price with good resale value.

If you are purchasing a house for the first time, starting with a smaller house you can comfortably afford is the best way to go. Then, when you are ready to move, you will do it comfortably.

Develop Financial Discipline!

We must be willing to adjust our lifestyles to come out

of difficult situations like excessive debt. When you work your way out of debt, you develop the needed discipline and money management to handle the harvest God has for you. You will need the discipline from this experience when God gets ready to bring you into your next experience.

God knows we make mistakes, but God's grace is sufficient. He will step in and show us His power by working miracles in our lives. When you are walking in God's will, and you are financially disciplined, you can make decisions based on God's will for your life.

The ultimate test of financial control—and this should be your goal, no matter your income—is when you can spend money, but you choose not to. That is the best indication that you have developed financial discipline. You may have some extra money to purchase what you want, but you choose not to because there is no need, and you are content with what you have.

Your objective should be to purchase items comfortably. If you're going to come out of debt, you must learn to purchase with a purpose. Extra finances do not justify bad stewardship. God is the greatest investor. If God keeps blessing you when you are unwise in handling money, God would be a bad investor. When you handle your money properly, you are setting yourself up for a harvest.

One thing I love about God is that until He brings you out of your situation, He will give you the grace to handle it. In 2 Corinthians 12:9, when Paul was experiencing an ongoing trial, the Lord told him, "'My grace is sufficient for you, for power is perfected in weakness.'" If you resolve to follow God's ways in your finances, He will bless your efforts and give you the grace to get through the hard stuff. You can always rely on that.

WORKBOOK

Chapter Four Questions

Question: What are some emotions of debt and how do they make it difficult to be practical and proactive? What are some emotional hindrances for you and/or your spouse that you need to set aside to seriously work on debt reduction? How has financial stress impacted your relationship with the Lord?

_____

_____

_____

_____

_____

_____

_____

_____

_____

_____

_____

_____

Question: Who in your life needs to know about your financial struggles, and who does not? How can you involve your children in the process of becoming debt-free? In what ways can you use your current difficulties as an opportunity to train them in money management? What do *you* need to learn now about financial discipline to give *them* the best possible foundation for their money management someday?

_____

_____

_____

_____

_____

_____

_____

_____

_____

_____

Question: *Until God brings you out of your situation, He will give you the grace to handle it. If you resolve to follow*

God's ways in your finances, He will bless your efforts and give you grace to get through the hard stuff. In what ways have you seen an extra measure of God's grace in your times of need? How has His grace sustained you in a season of want and enabled you to develop financial discipline?

_____
_____
_____
_____
_____
_____
_____
_____
_____
_____
_____

Take Action: *If you humble yourself, then that broke season will teach you some important lessons.* List some lessons, both practical and spiritual, you have learned or are learning, through a season of financial hardship. Are there ways in which going through financial hardship together has strengthened your relationship with your spouse?

Take Action: Weigh the benefits of cutting up your credit cards or taking them out of your wallet and keeping them in a drawer at home. If you plan to continue using them, write out some hard and fast rules that you will adhere to about when, why, and how much you can use your cards.

Take Action: Look at the six steps for rapid debt reduction. Which ones can you implement today? This week? This month? Write out a plan for how you will incorporate these steps into your budget.

Chapter Four Notes

CHAPTER FIVE

Building a Financial Future

Financial difficulty is one thing the devil uses to apply pressure to believers. He does this to distract us, disrupt us, and ultimately destroy us. Satan knows when you are consumed with debt and financial problems, you will have a hard time thinking about God's plan for you, "Set your mind on the things above, not on the things that are on earth" (Colossians 3:2). It's really hard to focus on heavenly things when the earthly things are getting you down.

Therefore, if Satan can keep you enslaved to debt, he can keep you distracted from your heavenly purpose. You need to let go of your pride, use the principles discussed in Chapter Four to get out of debt, and stop wasting your energy working two or three jobs to finance a lifestyle God did not promise you. When you make God the center of your life and handle your finances the way He commands you to, you'll build a real future for yourself and your family—financially and otherwise.

No matter what you're going through, you should have

hope, receive the joy of the Lord, and maintain that joy. You should be able to smile in the face of adversity because you see God's principles are working in your life. When you obey God in these areas and implement these principles, your harvest will come.

In this chapter, we'll look at a few ways you can lay a foundation for your future as you gain control over your finances. First, let's look a little more closely at the story of the widow from 2 Kings 4:1–7 that we studied in Chapter Four to see how we ought to trust God as we work to get out of debt.

A Prophet's Get-Out-of-Debt Process

You'll recall this is a short but powerful story about a widow who was threatened with the break-up of her family because of the debts her husband left her when he died. When she went to the prophet Elisha for help, he provided her with a debt removal plan that relied on God to perform a miracle. We may not always see a dramatic miracle like that which is described in this story, but you can be confident that when you obey God in faith, He'll move the mountains of debt in your life. The text of 2 Kings 4:1–2 demonstrates how faith works.

In verse 2 of this text, Elisha said to the woman, "How can I help you? Tell me, what do you have in your house?" (NIV). On the surface, that seemed like a strange question to ask a woman in so much debt that the creditors were threatening to sell her sons into slavery. She was broke and probably disgusted with her life. When you understand Scripture, you understand it is not so much that

Elisha needed the woman's offering—she told him all she had of value was a jar of oil—but that he was preparing her for a blessing.

Verse 3 says, "Go around and ask all your neighbors for empty jars. Don't ask for just a few" (NIV). The moment she identified what she had, he told her what to do. Notice Elisha's plan involved borrowing from her neighbors. Borrowing is not wrong—especially when you are doing it for the right reasons, and you do your homework—but excessive borrowing is wrong. In today's financial climate, it's crucial to remember lending institutions make money from the interest you pay. So, you never want to borrow flippantly or without careful thought and planning.

Therefore, when Elisha said, "Go around and ask all your neighbors for empty jars," it required faith for this widow to borrow jars. It also required faith for her neighbors to loan them to her. They knew she was struggling, and there was the possibility she would not bring the jars or the monetary equivalent back.

I think in our culture today when we can buy anything we need at the nearest Wal-Mart, we must remember vessels were made by hand from clay by the families who owned them. So, it was no small thing to lend someone a jar you had put time, effort, and raw materials into creating. If you didn't get that jar back, then that was several days of labor for you to make a new one. Both the widow and the neighbors needed faith with borrowing and lending out the jars.

Sometimes, God wants to give you more than you think He does, but He must stretch your faith before He can release your harvest. Jesus said, "It shall be done to you according to your faith" (Matthew 9:29). Some things that take place happen because God blesses us and honors the faith we have. The widow had to stretch her faith to receive the blessing God had for her.

In verse 4, Elisha said to "go inside and shut the door behind you and your sons" (NIV). In this situation, everybody in the house had to work. All of us have a responsibility to teach our children to have a high work ethic. And as we talked about in Chapter Four, the entire family was involved in this debt elimination.

Verse 5 says, "She left him and shut the door behind her and her sons. They brought the jars to her and she kept pouring" (NIV). She went into her house and followed Elisha's instructions to fix her problem. She put her faith into action. How many of us fail in our execution of God's commands? We are sent out each Sunday after we hear a sermon that could change our lives, but then return to our daily routine and never apply the principles discussed in the message. We not only need to believe what God says is true, but we need to act on it.

Verse 6 states, "When all the jars were full, she said to her son, 'Bring me another one.' But he replied, 'There is not a jar left.' Then the oil stopped flowing" (NIV). God will bless you to the extent of your ability to handle, hold, or house the blessing. You demonstrate your ability to do that by your past faithfulness to His commands. If you are not obedient, then you can't expect God to bless you.

Finally, in verse 7, it says, "She went and told the man of God, and he said, 'Go, sell the oil and pay your debts. You and your sons can live on what is left'" (NIV). This is where her life changed. Instead of blessing her with work for someone else, he put her in business.

This is what God did for the widow. She had borrowed those jars, and she still had valuable oil left over after she paid her debts. That means she had enough money to pay off *all* her debts, including the people from whom she borrowed the jars. Her life and her business became debt-free.

I pray you see this woman's story as something you can draw from and apply to your personal life. These spiritual directives for financial stability have been around for thousands of years as a source to help get us on the right track to financial freedom. We only need to read, trust, and obey them.

This story also shows us there is nothing wrong with wealth. It's how we go about obtaining it—and our motivations for doing so—when we choose to either obey God and live righteously, or disobey and fall into sin.

Build Wealth Honestly

God's grace in your life, the grace He will supply you with as you apply biblical principles to your finances, is not a license to do whatever you want, "Shall we sin because we are not under law but under grace? May it never be!" (Romans 6:15). We must never cut corners in our lives when it comes to right living, and that especially includes our finances.

Let's look at Proverbs 13:11 again, "Wealth obtained by fraud dwindles, but the one who gathers by labor increases it." Notice the word *labor* comes before the word *increase.* We often pounce on the word increase, but we are reluctant to talk about the labor involved in making that happen. You cannot have one without the other. Recall that one warning sign of debt was constantly looking for a get-rich-quick scheme. Many of those are fraudulent. Wealth was meant to be built slowly and with integrity.

The English Standard Version translates "the one who gathers by labor," in Proverbs 13:11, as "whoever gathers little by little." That is why the Bible tells us not to "despise these small beginnings" (Zechariah 4:10a NLT). Do not resent where God has you right now. You may only make minimum wage, but do not despise the day of small beginnings. What you do with a little will determine what you will do with a lot (Luke 16:10). Money is neither good nor bad; money instead reflects the character of the person who possesses it.

Above all else, be above reproach in your dealings with your finances (1 Timothy 3:2). Jesus said, "For what does it profit a man to gain the whole world, and forfeit his soul?" (Mark 8:36). You won't be doing yourself or your family any favors if you get yourself in a bad financial situation—or even worse, go to jail—because you got rich through theft or fraud. Don't even go there. Grow wealth God's way.

Four Keys to Build Your Financial Future

If you keep the following simple yet profound principles in mind, you will lay a good foundation for building wealth in your future.

1. Thankfulness

The apostle Paul said, "In everything give thanks; for this is God's will for you in Christ Jesus" (1 Thessalonians 5:18). He also says:

> *Not that I speak from want, for I have learned to be content in whatever circumstances I am. I know how to get along with humble means, and also know how to live in prosperity; in any and every circumstance I have learned the secret of being filled and going hungry, both of having abundance and suffering need. I can do all things through Him who strengthens me.*
> **—Philippians 4:11–13**

The key to financial stability is to learn how to be content. Thankfulness is not based on accumulating assets but on a positive attitude toward life. Don't feel like you have to buy that nice car your friend or family member just bought. You can be happy for them, but it has nothing to do with your household. You've got to learn to live on your level, so you can get to where God wants you to be.

Thankfulness is having the ability and wherewithal to serve God when your needs are not yet met and still declare, "My God is an awesome God." Either He's God or He's not, and we've got to learn how to trust Him even when we feel we can't see Him at work.

Everybody wants a miracle, but here's the problem—God has not called us to live off miracles; He's called us to live off principles. The principles are there to keep you from being in a position where you need a miracle. Therefore, whenever you see someone always in need of a miracle, that's somebody who's violating God's principles.

The Bible says, "The law of Your mouth is better to me than thousands of gold and silver pieces" (Psalm 119:72). The psalmist is essentially saying God is more precious to him than any wealth he has ever been given. When you can keep that perspective—treasuring God more than you treasure material possessions—you'll remain in a place of gratitude, and God can bless you.

2. Stewardship

Stewardship is the management of another's property, finances, or material goods. The stuff you own and accumulate isn't yours—it's God's. Even if you paid off your house, you really don't own it. When you die, you will leave it behind with the rest of your stuff. As the saying goes, hearses don't come with U-Hauls. They'll bury you in one suit with the back cut out! And because your stuff belongs to God, ultimately, you have to do what He wants you to with it.

It's important to have an eternal perspective on our temporary goods. You may have a lot of stuff, but your stuff shouldn't own you. When I understand it belongs to God, it's a lot easier to give it away and use it for His glory. You should want the Holy Spirit to guide you to save money so that you can solve others' problems and be a blessing to those in need. Cheap people are never happy people.

Stewardship is also being realistic about your current financial situation and planning accordingly. As we've discussed before, this is especially true when we are planning to get married. I often have couples coming to me wanting to get married when they're broke. One partner just lost a job, and the other person doesn't have one. But they will insist on the marriage because they're "in love." Love is great, but you can't eat love, and it doesn't keep the lights on. It doesn't buy diapers when you have kids. You will need more than love—you will need money, resources, and the wisdom to steward them well.

Keep in mind that your ability to be a couple that glorifies God together is not about how much money you earn, but the condition of your heart. If your lack of income results from laziness and poor stewardship—it's not the time to take on the additional responsibility of marriage and a family. It is possible when both members are willing to work hard and be good stewards of their finances, to be in a healthy, responsible marriage even if you have a lower income to start.

Stewardship is discussed all over the Bible. Luke 19:11–27, Jesus tells the Parable of the Ten Minas (a mina was a basic standard of weight among the ancient Hebrews. It was also used as currency or money):[18]

> *While they were listening to these things, Jesus went on to tell a parable, because He was near Jerusalem, and they supposed that the kingdom of God was going to appear immediately.*
>
> *So He said, "A nobleman went to a distant country to receive a kingdom for himself, and then return. And he called ten of his slaves, and gave them ten minas and said to them, 'Do business with this until I come back.' But his citizens hated him and sent a delegation after him, saying,*

'We do not want this man to reign over us.' When he returned, after receiving the kingdom, he ordered that these slaves, to whom he had given the money, be called to him so that he might know what business they had done.

"The first appeared, saying, 'Master, your mina has made ten minas more.' And he said to him, 'Well done, good slave, because you have been faithful in a very little thing, you are to be in authority over ten cities.' The second came, saying, 'Your mina, master, has made five minas.' And he said to him also, 'And you are to be over five cities.'

"Another came, saying, 'Master, here is your mina, which I kept put away in a handkerchief; for I was afraid of you, because you are an exacting man; you take up what you did not lay down and reap what you did not sow.'

"He said to him, 'By your own words I will judge you, you worthless slave. Did you know that I am an exacting man, taking up what I did not lay down and reaping what I did not sow? Then why did you not put my money in the bank, and having come, I would have collected it with interest?'

"Then he said to the bystanders, 'Take the mina away from him and give it to the one who has the ten minas.' And they said to him, 'Master, he has ten minas already.' I tell you that to everyone who has, more shall be given, but from the one who does not have, even what he does have shall be taken away. But these enemies of mine, who did not want me to reign over them, bring them here and slay them in my presence."

In the parable, the manager condemned the third man because he squirreled the money away. This was in disobedience to the manager because he had expected everyone to increase the money he had given them. This man did not have good stewardship.

Financial blessings are activated by giving—being generous with what God has given us—but they are maintained by stewardship. Giving and receiving and sowing and reaping are blessings maintained by our stewardship. When people struggle to get by daily, it is not because God did not meet their needs, but because they didn't properly manage what He gave them.

When you hit a financial crisis, you have to do one of two things. You have to increase your income or cut your spending. A lot of people don't like that second one. In extreme cases, you may have to do both. Sometimes stewardship looks like a drastic lifestyle change so you can get your priorities straight and your money under control.

So everything you accumulate in life is not yours; it's God's. Therefore, God reserves the right to call the shots in your life. If you really understand everything you have and will have results from His goodness and grace, then when He speaks to you, you'll be ready to respond in obedience. That is good stewardship.

3. Generosity

Generosity is the cure for greed. What you spend your money on indicates where your heart is:

> *"Do not store up for yourselves treasures on earth, where moth and rust destroy, and where thieves break in and steal. But store up for yourselves treasures in heaven, where neither moth nor rust destroys, and where thieves do not break in or steal; for where your treasure is, there your heart will be also."*
> **—*Matthew 6:19–21***

If you are willing to give your resources away to those who need them, you show the world and God that your treasure is in heaven, not on earth.

As I mentioned earlier in the book, Jesus said, "Give, and it will be given to you. They will pour into your lap a good measure—pressed down, shaken together, and running over. For by your standard of measure it will be measured to you in return" (Luke 6:38). God will bless you in proportion to how much you choose to bless others. Likewise, have you ever considered the blessing God sends into your life has got to come through somebody?

Praying for our needs is necessary, but we should want to be the answer to prayer to someone else's needs. The problem with the church is we have this mentality of always being on the receiving end of gifts. We're looking at the Scripture, praying for God to touch someone's heart, so they give us some money to meet our need. I learned this isn't the way God wants us to think. When I realized the blessing has to come from someone, I prayed, "God, make me the person! Since the blessing has to come through somebody, make me the man it comes through!" Don't you know that if water comes through a pipe, the pipe will get wet too? You will be blessed when you bless others.

When we look at getting our finances in order, we should look not only at the big house or fancy car we might afford someday, but also at how God might use us to help a family member through college, fund a missionary, or start a ministry. That's true generosity and good stewardship.

4. Work

Most of the world is doing everything it can to escape work and only play and relax, but as Christians, we must remember work is a gift from God. You've got to change your attitude about work to fit the biblical attitude toward it. Work should be one thing you look forward to every day for several reasons.

One, you should look forward to it because you're saved. When you're a Christian, and the Holy Spirit is working through you, He renews your mind to see things the way God sees them.

Two, you should look forward to work because God uses it to provide for you. Money doesn't fall out of the clouds. The normal way through which God provides for your needs is through your job.

Three, you should look forward to work because even before the curse came to the Garden of Eden, God gave Adam a job. He essentially said, "I want you to work the ground and make it productive" (Genesis 2:15). So God established work when the world was perfect, not as a result of the curse. Unfortunately, the enemy wants you to think your job is a curse, so you turn up to work with a negative attitude and never really get to where you want to be in life.

When you change your attitude, you change your destiny. It's important to work hard, not only when you are facing a review or your boss is breathing down your neck, but all the time (1 Thessalonians 4:11; Colossians 3:23–24). Your job should be a joy, and when you go to work with the right attitude, you can enjoy what you do.

If we Christians can follow God's ways of handling our finances, we will change our futures and build a legacy that benefits not only our families now but also our descendants down the line. Resolve to be remembered by those who come after you as someone faithful to the Lord and who gave from his or her resources generously. You'll help set a pattern for continued success for your family in the future.

WORKBOOK

Chapter Five Questions

Question: *If Satan can keep you enslaved to debt, he can keep you distracted from your heavenly purpose.* What are some ways debt or other financial obstacles have distracted you from God's purposes for your life? How can you turn your focus to an attitude of gratefulness for what you already have?

_____
_____
_____
_____
_____
_____
_____
_____
_____

_____

_____

Question: Think about the prayers you've prayed this week or this month. What was the focus of those prayers? Did your prayers focus more on what God or others could do for you? Or on ways you could become more like God through being a blessing to others? How does your prayer life and the posture of your heart need to change to better reflect generosity?

_____

_____

_____

_____

_____

_____

_____

_____

_____

_____

Question: Imagine standing before God tonight and giving an account of how you have stewarded every physical and financial resource He has given you. Does the thought make you nervous or excited? Would God say you have been a faithful steward? Why or why not? If not, what needs to change?

_____
_____
_____
_____
_____
_____
_____
_____
_____
_____
_____

Take Action: *You can be confident that when you obey God in faith, He'll move the mountains of debt in your life.* How is your financial need stretching your faith? Are you living by God's principles or looking for constant miracles? What are some practical ways you can exercise faith in God now, especially in this area of finances? List them and begin to implement them.

Take Action: Where is God calling you to be generous? Remember, generosity is a mindset. You can be generous with other resources besides money (e.g., inviting a family over for dinner, giving someone a ride in your car, helping an elderly or disabled person with chores that are too difficult for them). How will you demonstrate generosity this week?

Take Action: Each day this week, as you go to work, and as you leave work, thank the Lord for your job and giving you the physical and mental strength to work. Begin praying for your boss and coworkers. Ask God to give you His vision for why you are there and how you can be a witness for Him through a positive attitude and work ethic.

Chapter Five Notes

CHAPTER SIX

Maintaining Financial Freedom

How do you avoid sliding back into old habits once you have recognized your bad financial habits, corrected them, gotten rid of debt, budgeted your income, and changed your earthly attitude about giving and stewardship to a biblical one? How do you continue to build wealth and secure a good future for your family?

Adjusting to Life Without Debt: Seven Foundational Principles

If you have worked hard to get out of debt and get on firm financial footing, you'll never want to go back to the way things were when you were broke and stressed. If you are on the path God wants you to be on, you want to keep traveling that path and not drive off into a financial ditch, which will take even more work to get out of. These six principles should help you adjust to your new, debt-free life and maintain the financial freedom you have worked so hard for.

1. Keep Good Records

Have you ever put money into your bank account but didn't see it on your statement, or you had a different amount of money than the bank had? If you just go into complain, the bank can't do anything. But if you show your deposit receipt that proves they made a mistake, the bank has to correct it. When you're organized, structured, and hold onto important paperwork—like receipts, bank statements, and bills—it's a lot easier to keep track of your money and to catch any mistakes or discrepancies. If you are not disciplined to stay organized this way, you are not ready for the financial blessings God may have for you.

Remember when Jesus fed the five thousand (Matthew 14:13–21)? Before He performed the miracle of multiplying the loaves and fish, He told them to sit down in groups of fifty (Luke 9:14). He required order first. A lot of Christians think faith exempts them from exercising any discipline in their lives and handling their resources the right way. On the contrary, Christians should be the most organized and disciplined, especially with their finances.

2. Budgeting

We covered basic budging in chapter one, but essentially, budgeting is telling your money where to go instead of wondering where your money went. Budgeting not only helps you have enough money for your regular expenses, but it also helps you prepare for emergencies or fun things like Christmas and vacations. When you have budgeted money for these eventualities, you'll be a lot less stressed and less likely to hit a financial crisis or overspend.

3. Saving

Everybody's budget should include a section for saving. If you're living from paycheck to paycheck, not saving, and your job fires you tomorrow, how will you function without that income? Every financial expert will tell you that you need at least six to seven months' worth of your salary in a savings account to protect you and your family from financial devastation. You will have to live in your future, so you want to have a future you've prepared for.

4. Tithing

None of these other principles will work if you are not tithing part of your income. The Bible suggests ten percent, but God may want you to tithe fifteen or twenty percent. At some points in your life, five percent might make more sense. The point is, don't hold back your money from God. Be a cheerful giver (2 Corinthians 9:7). Commit first to giving to your local church, and then find other ministries and causes you find important and give to them too.

5. Contentment

Contentment and gratitude go hand in hand. You can enjoy life on a small income. It amazes me how Christians who know their Bible have a meltdown when they run into some financial difficulty. You just have to give up some stuff, that's all. You haven't lost your salvation; you haven't lost Christ. You can't lose those things, and that is what is most important. If you don't have Jesus, you don't have anything. So keep financial difficulties in perspective.

Contentment is a learned behavior. You have to choose to be content. Discontentment happens when you look over at somebody else instead of focusing on what you've got and being content with that. Just because something looks good doesn't mean it's good for you. If we learn to be content no matter what state we're in, we will be more secure in our finances.

Let's say you're a single mother. Don't feel like you need to have a huge house with a three-car garage. You need to live comfortably and provide for your kids until God blesses you with the next level, whatever that is. And then be content there too.

When you figure out your money and learn to be content with whatever financial situation God has you in, it will be better for your family and your church. You'll be a better giver, and you'll have better health because you won't be worried about money all the time. You have to find your value and identity in Christ and not in your net worth.

You've got to come to grips with your situation and

say, "It is what it is." Let's start from where we are, put together a plan, and walk toward increase.

6. Spending Less

When you get a raise or a bonus this year, don't raise your spending. Proverbs 13:22 says, "A good man leaves an inheritance to his children's children." You can't leave anything if you have nothing. Save excess or unexpected income instead of immediately blowing it on the latest new thing you've had your eye on. You can do a lot more with a lot less if you're clever, careful, and disciplined in your spending.

7. Avoid Surety

Surety is the biblical word for co-signing on a loan. Essentially this happens when someone is attempting to purchase something that is above their means and requires taking out a loan. This could be for a vehicle or even a house. A person requires a co-signer when they didn't get approved for a loan, usually due to a low credit score—which may indicate a poor history managing finances.

Whenever you co-sign for something, you're putting your financial health at the risk of somebody else's character. Proverbs 11:15 says, "He who is a guarantor for a stranger will surely suffer for it, but he who hates being a guarantor is secure."

It's hard enough sometimes to run your own house, let alone be responsible for someone else's. Therefore, it's really important to learn that if you violate that biblical financial principle, you'll suffer loss. Don't waste all of your hard work becoming financially stable by letting someone else's irresponsibility drag you back to financial ruin.

Financial Freedom Is Possible

If you've done the hard work to get to a place of financial freedom, it'll take a little work to stay there, but it's worth it in the long run. Imagine entering a marriage on stable footing, ready to buy that house, or have children without the worry. Imagine improving your marriage and leaving a legacy for your children. All those things are possible, but it takes discipline, hard work, and a lifestyle change. You can do it with God's help.

WORKBOOK

Chapter Six Questions

Question: How are you doing at sticking to your budget? Has it been freeing to have everything allotted, or difficult to discipline yourself to stick to the plan? Do you need to make adjustments to your budget to make it more practical? How can you keep yourself motivated to continue sticking to a budget even after your financial situation improves?

_____

_____

_____

_____

_____

_____

_____

_____

_____

_____

_____

Question: What are your goals for a short-term and long-term savings? How are you doing in working toward those goals? Are you disciplined in saving rather than spending extra or unexpected income?

_____

_____

_____

_____

_____

_____

_____

_____

_____

_____

Question: Are you a content person? In what areas are you tempted to not be content, to want more than what God has given? Ask God to help you be creative, thankful, industrious, and faithful right where He has you. What can you do to grow in your contentment with the life you have? Why is contentment so vital for marriage?

_____
_____
_____
_____
_____
_____
_____
_____
_____
_____
_____

Take Action: Set an appointment with yourself (or with your spouse if you are married) and spend a morning or afternoon getting all your financial paperwork in order. Decide if you will keep hard copies, electronic copies, or both; if you will use financial software and what type; and how you will sort and remember outstanding bills. Keep your systems simple and user-friendly.

Take Action: If you have not been tithing to your local church, plan now how you will start giving this Sunday. If you are tithing, ask God to show you needs in your church or community that you can help meet.

Chapter Six Notes

CONCLUSION

Financial Freedom

We've covered a lot of ground, and I hope you have found not only some practical tools you can use *today* to improve your financial situation but also more than that, I hope you've gained a better understanding of God's plan for your finances.

Money is temporary. You can't take any of it, or the stuff you bought, with you when you die. When we put money in the place of God and worship it, then our lives will be painful and difficult. When we put God in His proper place in our lives, and look at our money as a way to serve Him and others, we will make better choices, and He will bless us. We may not die millionaires, but we will have given our families an example to carry on through their lives. We will leave a legacy and witness to God's faithfulness in our lives.

The focus of this book was how money affects our families. If you are not yet married, I urge you again to get your finances in order before you marry your spouse. Get a steady job, pay your bills on time, and get out of and stay out of debt. Be the excellent woman or virtuous man God calls you to be. Be worthy of the good spouse that you are praying for.

If you are already married, and you feel like your life is a mess because you've made bad financial decisions, hope is not lost! Show your family you have integrity by applying the principles in this book and from the Bible to your life. Pray God changes your attitude and thinking about material wealth, debt, contentment, and gratitude. If you do that, you will see real change and might even pull your family back from crisis.

A lot of resources are out there to help you with all the nitty-gritty of the topics we've covered in this book, including debt, budgeting, purchasing a home, work, and investing. Be a student of money. Above all else, go to the Bible for help. The Bible is never outdated, and it is always right. You can always trust the principles and commands God gives in it are relevant for your situation and can help you follow His ways for your life (2 Timothy 3:16–17).

My prayer is that every reader finds financial freedom and success. You may look crazy to the world when you make hard decisions with your money, but you will reap the benefits and so will your family. Don't be afraid to get started now on the beautiful life God has for you.

About the Author

Pastor John F. Ramsey Sr. is the gifted and anointed founder and senior pastor of New Life Worship Center, an exciting and rapidly growing church located in Indianapolis, Indiana. He ministers with power while using humor to make often complex biblical concepts enjoyable, simple, relevant, and practical.

Pastor Ramsey attended Fort Wayne public schools and graduated from Snider High School. Following graduation, inspired by his love of athletics, he accepted a football scholarship at Miami University of Ohio and began pursuing a major in education. During his junior year, at the age of twenty-one, he accepted God's call to the ministry. It was during these college years when he began readying himself to do God's will on a full-time basis.

In 2001, God called Pastor Ramsey and his wife, Alicia, to open the New Life Worship Center with the help of Eastern Star Church. Pastor Ramsey developed a central theme for New Life Worship Center: *"A Local Church with a Global Vision."* Pastor Ramsey and the New Life Worship Center family are fully positioned to reach God's people on a local, regional, national, and international basis.

As it grew, New Life Worship Center moved from its initial, 350-seat sanctuary (Kessler location) into a new main location—a 13-acre, 80,000-square-foot, 1,400-seat facility in the city's historic Traders Point neighborhood—in July 2005. Since its inception, the church has grown to over 5,000 members with thirty active ministries. To more effectively serve the Indianapolis community, in 2007, New Life Worship Center also completed the cash purchase of a central campus location at 3425 Boulevard Place in Center Township.

Pastor Ramsey serves as a mentor and spiritual father to a number of local pastors. He is blessed to serve under Bishop I.V. Hilliard of New Light Christian Center in Houston, Texas, as his spiritual father. Pastor Ramsey is a much sought-after preacher and a featured national keynote speaker for various leadership and development programs. He is a member of the Association of

Independent Ministries. God's anointing has enabled Pastor Ramsey to bring some of the nation's leading pastors, teachers, and recording artists to New Life Worship Center to bless the congregation and the Indianapolis community each year. He also consults at Taylor University regarding diversity and leadership and as a ministry mentor.

Pastor Ramsey is most passionate about helping families to become stronger. Known for his anointing in the areas of faith, relationships, and financial stewardship, he is the author of *Smart Money Management*, *Armed and Dangerous*, and *One Night Stand*. He is also the co-author of a highly regarded book entitled *About My Father's Business: Merging Industry and Ministry*.

Pastor Ramsey is married to his lovely wife, Alicia, and they are the proud parents of three wonderful children: a daughter, Judah Maree, and sons Jeremiah David and John Jr.

REFERENCES

Notes

[1] Park, Brandon. "2,350 Bible Verses on Money." Church Leaders. November 30, 2017. https://churchleaders.com/outreach-missions/outreach-missions-articles/314227-2350-bible-verses-money.html.

[2] "Household Debt and Credit Report (Q1 2019)." Federal Reserve Bank of New York: Center for Microeconomic Data. https://www.newyorkfed.org/microeconomics/hhdc.html.

[3] Guzman, Gloria G. "Household Income: 2017." United States Census Bureau. September 2018. https://www.census.gov/library/publications/2018/acs/acsbr17-01.html.

[4] Bishaw, Alemayehu and Craig Benson. "Poverty: 2016 and 2017." United States Census Bureau. September 2018. https://www.census.gov/library/publications/2018/acs/acsbr17-02.html.

[5] *ESV Study Bible.* Crossway, 2001.

[6] Mandayal, Suchayan. "Colonel Sanders Founded KFC at the Age of 65! Here's His Incredible True Story." Business Insider. https://www.businessinsider.in/colonel-sanders-founded-kfc-at-the-age-of-65-heres-his-incrediblyinspiring-story/articleshow/55773640.cms.

[7] Lake, Rebecca. "23 Dizzying Average American Savings Statistics." Credit Donkey. May 18, 2016. https://www.creditdonkey.com/average-american-savings-statistics.html.

[8] See Ramsey, Dave. "EveryDollar." Dave Ramsey. https://www.daveramsey.com/everydollar.

[9] Shaw, Gabbi. "These Are the 11 Most Common Reasons People Get Divorced, Ranked." Insider. January 31, 2019. https://www.insider.com/why-people-get-divorced-2019-1.

[10] "Virtuous." Meriam-Webster. https://www.merriam-webster.com/dictionary/virtuous.

[11] Regalado-Garcia, Avelynn. "Be Seed-Minded than Need-Minded." CBN-Asia. https://cbnasia.org/home/2012/07/be-seed-minded-than-need-minded/.

[12] Stanley, Thomas J. *The Millionaire Mind.* Andrews McMeel Publishing, 2001.

[13] Harrison, R. K., Ronald F. Youngblood, and F. F. Bruce. *Nelson's Illustrated Bible Dictionary.* Rev. edition. Thomas Nelson, 2014, p. 1103.

[14] Cole, Edwin Louis. "Coleisms." Ed Cole Library. https://www.edcole.org/index.php?fuseaction=coleisms.show Coleism&id=271&keywords=viewall&page=28.

[15] Cole, Edwin Louis. *Maximized Manhood Study Guide.* Harrison House, 1985.

[16] O'Connell, Brian. "What's the Average U.S. Credit Card Debt by Income and Age in 2019?" The Street. February 16, 2019. https://www.thestreet.com/personal-finance/credit-cards/average-credit-card-debt-14863601.

[17] See Oral Roberts, "3 Keys to the Seed Faith Principle." https://inspiration.org/christian-articles/seed-faith-principle/.

[18] "Mina." Encyclopaedia Britannica. https://www.britannica.com/science/mina-unit-of-weight.

www.ingramcontent.com/pod-product-compliance
Lightning Source LLC
Chambersburg PA
CBHW060032180426
43196CB00045B/2631